THE LION
READ & KNOW
BIBLE

SOPHIE PIPER ILLUSTRATED BY ANTHONY LEWIS

LION
CHILDREN'S

Contents

To

From

For Kathryn, Isabella, Emilia and Rory   A.L.

Text by Sophie Piper
Illustrations copyright © 2008 Anthony Lewis
This edition copyright © 2016 Lion Hudson

Published by Lion Children's Books
an imprint of
Lion Hudson plc
Wilkinson House, Jordan Hill Road,
Oxford OX2 8DR, England
www.lionhudson.com/lionchildrens
ISBN 978 0 7459 4996 3
ISBN 978 0 7459 7639 6 (midi hardback)
ISBN 978 0 7459 7659 4 (paperback)

First edition 2008
First midi hardback edition 2016
First paperback edition 2016

A catalogue record for this book is available
from the British Library

Printed and bound in China, November 2015, LH25

The New Testament   228

THE OLD TESTAMENT is the first part of the Christian Bible. Its ancient stories tell of the Jewish people and the God they believed in.

It tells of the laws God gave to the people in the time of Moses. By obeying these laws, they believed, they would truly be God's holy people.

All too often, they failed. But as the years went by, they came to understand that their holy God was also a God of love and forgiveness.

Old Testament

The making of the world

Genesis 1–2

Before the beginning there was nothing: a huge, dark nothing.

A huge dark nothing – and God.

God spoke aloud to the darkness: 'Let there be light.'

And the light came spinning and sparkling from the nowhere.

'That is good,' said God. 'That is very good.

'Now there will be light as well as dark; there will be day and night.

'And this has been the very first day.'

On the second day, God called out again: 'Let the sky spread as far as far can go.'

The most beautiful sky rolled across the everywhere.

On the third day, God spoke again: 'Let there be land and let there be sea.'

From beneath the rippling water arose tall
mountains and rolling hills.

'Now I want seedlings to uncurl from the earth and
to clothe the earth in green and gold,' said God.

And so it was.

On the fourth day, God told the sun to shine brightly. That night, God told the moon to float across the sky while the stars twinkled all around.

As the fifth day dawned, God spoke again: 'Let there be fish in the sea and birds in the air.

'Let there be animals for the fields and animals for the forests.'

And all the creatures began to awaken – some scaly, some feathery, some furry. Each one was different. Each one was special.

As the sun rose on the sixth day, God spoke again: 'Today I am making humankind. They will be my friends. This world will be their home.'

God smiled at the people – at the man and at the woman – and they smiled back.

Then, on the seventh day, God rested.

'I am pleased,' said God. 'Everything is very, very good.'

Places in the Old Testament

The stories of the Old Testament are centred on the land of
Canaan. It was here that the people of Israel made their home.
The stories unfold over hundreds of years. Over that time, some
places had different names. This map is simply to help you find
the setting of the stories in this book.

GREECE

CRETE

The Philistines who invaded
Canaan may have sailed
from here.

Mediterranean Sea

River N

EGYPT

Joseph brought the
people of Israel to Egypt.

MOUNT ARARAT

The Bible story says Noah's ark landed on Mount Ararat.

PERSIA

ASSYRIA

Nineveh

The garden of Eden story is set between the Tigris and Euphrates.

River Tigris

River Euphrates

Babylon

BABYLONIA

MOUNT CARMEL

CANAAN

River Jordan

Joppa

Shiloh

Jericho

Jerusalem

Bethlehem

Philistine cities

MOAB

Midianites

The area shown in bright green is sometimes called the Fertile Crescent – the area best for farming.

SINAI

Moses received the Law on Mount Sinai.

The garden of Eden

Genesis 2–3

The first man God made was called Adam. The first woman God made was called Eve. God planted a beautiful garden in Eden where they could live.

'Everything here is for you to enjoy,' said God, 'and everything is good. But take care: in the middle of the garden is a tree that is a rogue. You must not eat its fruit. If you do, you will find out about all the bad things that could spoil this good world.'

Adam and Eve were happy to do as God wanted, and all was well in their paradise home.

One day, a snake slithered up to Eve.

'I can't believe what God said to you!' whispered the snake. 'That tree in the middle of the garden is simply beautiful. Its fruit won't hurt you.'

'Oh yes it will,' replied Eve. 'It's a rogue. That's what God said.'

The snake wound itself a little closer. 'I'll tell you a secret,' it said. 'Its fruit will make you wise. Eat it, and you will simply be as wise as God.'

Eve went closer to the tree. Its plump, ripe fruit looked very tempting.

'Just a little taste, then,' she said.

She picked one of the fruit and bit into it. 'It's delicious,' she said. 'Adam, come and try this fruit.'

Adam came, and he ate it, and he smiled as he munched.

Then all at once, Adam and Eve knew: they had disobeyed God. They hardly dared look at each other for shame. They knew they must hide from God.

That evening, God came into the garden to talk with them, as friends do.

God found out what had happened, and God spoke in a voice that was heavy with sadness. 'Adam and Eve, you have disobeyed me. You have chosen to know about bad things.

'So now you must leave this paradise garden. In the world beyond, the badness is already growing… there are thorns and thistles, there is death and decay.

'Out there you will have to work long and hard for the crops you need. Life will seem cruelly hard.'

Then God sent a fierce angel to guard the way into Paradise. Would human beings ever have a way back?

Noah and the flood

Genesis 6–9

After God made man and woman, years and years went by. There were people living all over the world.

God looked at them and was sad. 'They have let badness grow like weeds,' said God. 'They do nothing but quarrel and fight.

'There is only one person who is good and kind. His name is Noah, and I am going to ask him to help me put the world to rights.'

So God went to speak to Noah.

'I want you to build me a boat,' said God. 'An enormous ark.

'It's not an ark that is just for you. It's not an ark that is just for your family. It must be an ark that is big enough for a mother and father of every kind of creature.

'When it is ready, I am going to send a flood to wash the bad old world away.'

Noah did as God told him.

His three sons Shem, Ham and Japheth worked hard to help him.

Noah's wife and his sons' wives were as busy as could be.

Soon it was time to bring the animals down from the mountain tops and out of the forest glades onto the ark.

When they were all safe on board, God shut the door.

Then it began to rain. It rained and rained as never before.

The flood rose above the houses. It rose above the trees. It rose above the mountain tops.

In all the world there was only Noah and his amazing ark.

And rain.

The days and weeks went by, grey and dreary.

Then the rain stopped and the wind began to blow. The ark drifted along in the rippling water, until one day…

Crrr…unch! The ark rocked and then stood still.

'We've hit land!' cried Noah. 'This is every sailor's nightmare.'

He paused for a moment. 'But we're not sailors. We're survivors. It's good news, everyone! The flood must be going down.'

Not long after, mountain tops began to appear like tiny islands. Noah let out a raven, and it flew and flew and kept on flying. Noah did not know where it went.

'But we need to know if there's land,' said Noah. 'I shall send a dove to look.'

The dove flew high and far away… but as the sun dipped low, it came flying back to the ark.

Seven days later, Noah set it free again. This time, it came back with a fresh green olive leaf in its beak. Everyone was delighted! Somewhere, not too far away, new life was springing up from the oozing mud.

Seven days after that, when Noah let the dove go free, it flew away and didn't come back. The flood was over.

At last, the land was dry.

'It's time for you and all the creatures to leave the ark,' said God.

'I want you all to begin the world again.'

The birds flew away, trilling to the heavens.

The animals leaped and ran and shuffled and crept through the fresh green grass. They were eager to find new homes and have new families.

Noah and his family laughed for joy. 'Thank you, God,' they cried. 'Thank you for keeping us safe.'

Then, all at once, a beautiful rainbow arched across the sky.

'Look!' said God. 'The rainbow is the sign of my promise. Never again will I flood the world. There will be summer and winter, seedtime and harvest, day and night for ever.'

A fertile land

People and nations make their home in places that have good harvests. It is no surprise that the Bible stories are set in a region between the Mediterranean Sea and the dry desert, where there is enough rainfall for wild plants and crops to thrive.

FOREST AND HILLSIDE

Pine

Oak

Cedar of Lebanon

Olive

Vine

Vegetables in a watered garden

36

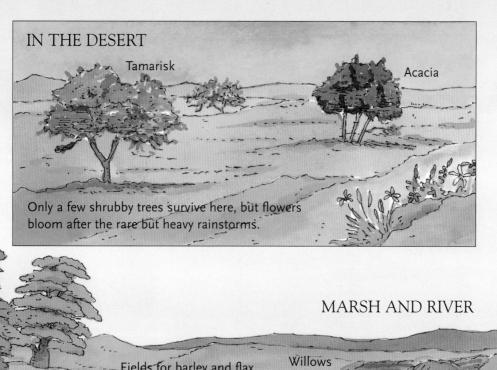

IN THE DESERT

Tamarisk

Acacia

Only a few shrubby trees survive here, but flowers bloom after the rare but heavy rainstorms.

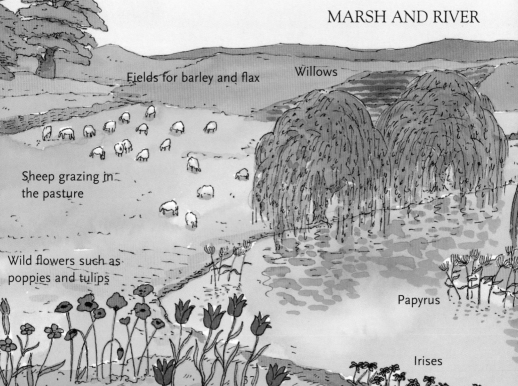

MARSH AND RIVER

Fields for barley and flax

Willows

Sheep grazing in the pasture

Wild flowers such as poppies and tulips

Papyrus

Irises

Abraham and the starry sky

Genesis 12, 15, 17–18, 21, 24

Long ago, in the land of Canaan, lived a wealthy man. One day, he was sitting and watching the sun go down. Everything looked perfect in its rosy light.

'It was God who told me to come to this land,' Abram said to himself, 'and God has blessed me.

'I have silver and gold. I have sheep and goats and cattle. I have servants to work for me: they take the flocks to pasture and fetch water for them from the wells.

'And my wife is the most beautiful woman in the land.'

Then, all at once, the light faded and everything went grey.

'But we have no children,' he sighed. 'And my wife and I are growing old. So, all that I have will come to nothing.'

Then, in the twilight, God came and God spoke.

'Come! Look at the sky and try to count the stars.'

Abram looked up. Night was falling. The stars were beginning to twinkle… more and more of them in a sky that seemed to go on for ever.

'I'll never be able to count them all,' laughed the man.

'Listen,' said God. 'I am making you a promise.

You and your wife are going to be parents… then
grandparents… then great-grandparents. Your family
will grow and grow as the years go by. Just as it is
impossible to count the stars, so it will be impossible
to count how many people there are in your family.

'I will be their God; they will be my people. They
will bring my blessing to all the world.'

'Keep listening,' said God. 'I am going to give you new names. Yours will be Abraham. Your wife's will be Sarah.

'She will have a son, and you will name him Isaac.

'Tonight, you are both sad that you don't have children. But when your son is born, you will laugh for joy.'

And indeed, Abraham and Sarah were delighted with their baby son.

When Isaac grew up, he married a woman named Rebecca.

Whenever Abraham saw the stars come out in the sky above, he believed with all his heart that God's promises were coming true.

Nomads

From the time Abraham set out for the land of Canaan, he and his family were nomads. They remained so until the time of Joseph, when they moved to Egypt and settled there. When Moses led the people back to Canaan, once again they lived a nomadic life.

The tentcloth is woven from goat's hair.

A curtain divides the tent into a room and a 'porch'.

Woven cloth is one of the things nomads can make to sell.

Donkeys are used t[o] carry heavy loads.

Servants dig a well.

Nomads make camp when they find pasture for their flocks, but move on when it is used up.

Nomads do not grow crops and need to trade.

45

Jacob and his brother Esau

Genesis 25, 27–33

Jacob was the son of Isaac and Rebecca.

He was not the only son: he had a twin brother named Esau. Esau was the older of the two. He was tall and strong and he liked exploring the outdoors. His father admired him greatly.

Jacob liked to stay at home. That pleased Jacob's mother, but the young man felt that he was always second best to Esau. He dreamed of getting even.

Even if I have to cheat, he thought to himself.

One day, when they were grown up, Esau came home from hunting feeling very hungry.

Jacob had stayed at home, cooking. He was stirring a pot of soup.

'I need soup NOW,' declared Esau.

'You can have some,' said Jacob, 'but on one condition. From now on, I want to be treated as the eldest son round here.'

'Oh, fine,' said Esau. 'I don't care.'

More years passed. The twins' father, Isaac, grew old and blind.

'Esau,' he called. 'I want you to go hunting. I want you to make me a good meat stew with what you catch. Then I will say the blessing prayer for you before I die.'

Esau went off with his bow and arrows. The twins' mother, Rebecca, came hurrying to Jacob.

'Come now,' she whispered, 'so you can get even with Esau. We must make a meat stew. You must take it to your father and ask him to say the blessing prayer for you.'

She helped Jacob to dress up so that his clothes and even his skin felt like Esau's.

Jacob brought the stew to his father – and he fooled the old man into believing he was Esau. Jacob smiled as he listened to the blessing prayer. Isaac was asking God to give him so many good things. Now he would surely do better than Esau.

When Esau came home, he found out what had happened.

'I've been cheated,' he cried. 'I could kill my brother!'

There was such an uproar that Rebecca was afraid for her younger son. She asked Isaac to let Jacob go to her own brother's home, far away.

It was a good plan, but Jacob still felt lonely and downhearted as he went along. After a day's walk, he lay down on the dusty earth to sleep.

As he slept, he had a dream. He saw a giant stairway reaching from earth to heaven, and angels going up and coming down. Then God spoke.

'I will bless you and keep you safe,' said God.

'You will have children and grandchildren.
Tonight you are sleeping on dusty ground –
it would be hard to count the specks of
dust. One day, it will be harder to
count how many people there
are in your family.'

Rebecca's brother was called Laban. He welcomed the young man into his household. A whole month went by.

'I'd like to stay,' said Jacob to his uncle, 'because I've fallen in love. Please, let me work for you for seven years. Then, in return, I would like to marry your beautiful daughter, Rachel.'

Laban agreed, and Jacob worked hard, looking after his uncle's flocks of sheep and goats.

At last, his wedding day came. His bride arrived, lovely in her wedding clothes and smiling shyly through her veil.

When they were husband and wife, Jacob saw her face to face.

'You tricked me!' he cried to Laban. 'This is Rachel's sister, Leah.'

Laban shrugged. 'She's my elder daughter,' he said. 'It's the custom here to make sure the elder daughter marries first. But the custom allows you more than one wife. Next week, you can marry Rachel.'

He smiled, and Jacob saw that he was looking smug. 'You'll have to work for me seven more years, of course,' said Laban.

Jacob knew he had been tricked, and he wanted to get even.

When the next seven years were over, he went again to Laban. 'I'd like to take my family and go off on my own,' he said.

'Dear boy,' replied Laban, 'that would be a shame. We've grown wealthy because of all you've done. Why not name your wages and stay?'

'Fair enough,' said Jacob. 'Let me go on taking care of your flocks. For pay, I will have just the speckled or spotted goats and the black sheep.'

The two men agreed on the deal. As the years went by, Jacob made sure that many speckled and spotted kids and black lambs were born.

That made him a wealthy man – rich enough to take good care of his growing family.

But something else had happened too: he had found out how cheating gets in the way of being friends. Esau wasn't friends with him; he wasn't friends with Laban.

In the end, he made an agreement with his uncle.

'Let me go back to my home country,' he said, 'and let us put our quarrels behind us.' Laban agreed.

Before they went their separate ways, Laban kissed his daughters and his grandchildren goodbye.

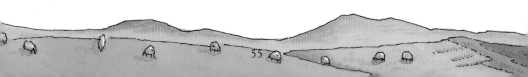

Jacob was glad to be going to his home country – but he was anxious too. He wanted to be friends with his brother again… but he didn't know if Esau wanted to be friends with him.

Then, one night, a strange thing happened. A stranger came and fought with Jacob – someone he struggled to beat.

Jacob demanded that the stranger say a blessing prayer for him.

'All your life, you have been fighting me and other people,' said the stranger. 'Now the struggle is over, and you have triumphed. From now on, you are a new person with a new name: Israel.'

As day dawned, Jacob-named-Israel understood: he had seen God face to face and lived to tell the tale.

That very day, Esau arrived with his fighting men. It was easy to see that he had grown rich and powerful.

Jacob bowed low.

Esau simply hugged him. 'Let's forget the quarrels of the past,' he said.

The brothers were friends at last.

Joseph and his brothers

Genesis 37

Jacob – whom God called Israel – had twelve sons.

Their names were Reuben, Simeon, Levi, Judah, Dan, Naphtali, Gad, Asher, Issachar, Zebulun, Joseph and Benjamin.

Reuben was the eldest.

Benjamin was the youngest.

Joseph was his father's favourite. Jacob had his reasons: after all, Joseph was the elder son of Rachel – the wife Jacob loved most.

But this did not mean much to Joseph's brothers, and they were not happy.

They were even less happy when Jacob gave Joseph a magnificent coat.

'It's not the style I mind,' said Reuben, 'and it's not the pattern in blue and red and purple and gold.

'It's what it means: that Joseph is going to be treated as the eldest, with all kinds of privileges.'

Joseph didn't make things easier for anyone.

'Listen,' he said to his brothers one day. 'I had a dream and we were all in it. We were tying up sheaves of wheat. My sheaf stood up straight. Your sheaves came and bowed down to it.'

'Dream on!' the brothers sneered. 'We're never going to bow to you.'

Joseph swaggered away in his fancy coat.

Not long after, he had another dream. 'Listen to this,' he said to his family. 'In this dream, the sun, the moon and eleven stars came and bowed down to me.'

What he said made Jacob angry. 'Do you think that I and your mother and all your brothers are going to bow down to you?' he scolded. 'Joseph – you are going too far.'

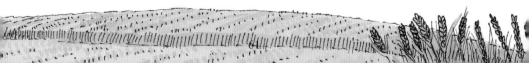

Not long after that, the brothers went off to find pasture for the family flocks. When they had been gone some time, Jacob sent Joseph to make sure that they were safe.

The brothers saw him coming and began to grumble. 'Here's the dreamer – the one who wants to boss us all around,' they muttered.

'Why don't we get rid of him? For ever.'

They agreed on a plan. When Joseph came close, they jumped on him, ripped off his fancy coat and threw him in a dry well. Reuben did not want the punishment to turn to disaster, and he planned to rescue Joseph. The others sat down to enjoy their meal.

They were laughing and joking about what they had
done.

As they ate, they saw some traders heading for
Egypt. Their camels were laden with precious goods
to sell in the markets there.

'Let's sell Joseph,' the brothers agreed. 'He can be
a slave in Egypt.'

So they pulled him from the well and sold him to
the traders.

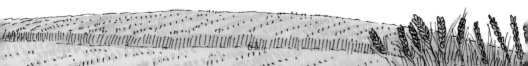

Reuben was dismayed when he found out what had
happened. Even so, he agreed to help cover up the
wicked thing his brothers had done. They took
Joseph's coat and dipped it in the blood of an animal.

'We will take this to our father,' they agreed. 'We
will say it is all we have left of Joseph. We will make
him think he was killed and eaten by a wild animal.'

Jacob believed their story and he wept bitterly.

In faraway Egypt, a wealthy man named Potiphar
bought Joseph.

'He's young and strong,' he said to himself. 'I think
he will be very useful.'

Wild creatures

Long ago, fierce animals hunted for prey throughout the Bible lands. Many of these creatures are now extinct in the region.

DAWN

A vulture waits for scraps of flesh.

Ravens

Jackals look greedily at tasty sheep.

Sparrows

Owl

DUSK

Many animals come out in the half light.

Fox

The wolf pack trots through the woods.

Quail

A brown bear sniffs for ripe fruit.

Lions and leopards wait for deer and gazelle coming to drink at the river.

Doves

Joseph and the dream

Genesis 39–46

Joseph was all alone. He was far from home. He was a slave in a foreign land with no one to protect him.

Except God.

Joseph put his trust in God, and soon things began to go well.

His master, Potiphar, was very pleased with his work. In time, he put him in charge of his household.

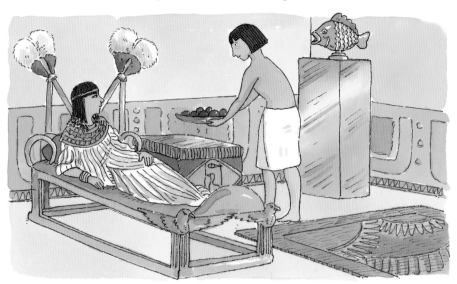

Then came trouble: Potiphar's wife asked Joseph to do things that were disloyal to his master.

When Joseph said no, she told lies about him and had him thrown into prison.

Joseph was all alone again. He was a prisoner with no one to protect him.

Once again, he put his trust in God.

He made himself so useful in the prison that the jailer put him in charge of the other prisoners.

They liked him because he was fair. They liked him because he was wise. They liked him because he could explain the meaning of dreams.

Joseph could do this for one reason only: God helped him to see all that was going to happen.

He was gentle when the dreams meant he had bad news to tell; he was happy when the dreams meant he had good news.

One of the prisoners who had a good news dream was the king's butler.

'The king is going to pardon you,' Joseph told him. 'He will set you free and let you be his butler again.

'When that happens, please put in a good word for me. I haven't done anything wrong, so I don't deserve to stay in prison.'

Not long after, the butler was back in his old job, serving wine to the king.

But sadly, he forgot all about Joseph.

He didn't think about him at all… until the day the king himself had a puzzling dream.

'None of my wise men can explain it,' complained the king. 'Is there no one who can help?'

Then the butler remembered. 'I know someone who understands dreams,' he said. 'His name's Joseph. He's in the royal prison.'

The king sent for Joseph at once.

'Listen,' he said to the young man. 'Here is my dream. I was on the river bank. Seven cows came up out of the river. They were fat and sleek, and they began grazing on the lush green grass.

'Then seven more cows came out of the river. They were thin and bony, and they ate the fat cows greedily. But it was no use: they stayed as thin and bony as before.

'Then I had another dream. I saw seven ears of corn – all plump and ripe and golden.

'Then seven more ears sprouted. They were shrivelled and dry. They swallowed up the good corn.

'The dreams have got me worried. What do they say about the future?'

'My God can help me explain,' said Joseph. 'The two dreams mean the same thing. There are going to be seven years of good harvests and then seven years of bad harvests.

'To avoid disaster, you will need to find someone wise. That person must save extra corn in the good years. Then your people will have food to eat in the bad years.'

The king did not take long to make his plan. 'I shall put you in charge,' he told Joseph.

All at once, Joseph was the second most powerful person in all Egypt. He was given a golden chariot to ride in, and wherever he went, people bowed down.

Joseph ordered barns to be built.

He ordered people to bring their spare corn to the barns. For seven years, they had plentiful crops, and the barns were filled.

The next year, the crops failed. The people came to Joseph to buy corn, and there was plenty to sell.

Soon, people from the lands beyond Egypt came begging to buy corn.

One day, ten men came. Their faces were thin and their clothes drooped on their skinny bodies.

As they bowed low, Joseph suddenly knew.

These were his ten older half brothers. And he wanted more than anything to hear news of his younger brother: his one true brother, Benjamin.

Joseph did not say who he was, and the brothers did not recognize him. Joseph asked lots of questions about his family and listened to what the brothers were saying to each other in their own language. He found out that they were sorry for what they had done to him.

Then he made a plan. 'You can have corn,' he said, 'but one of you must stay here. The rest must go and fetch the youngest brother, Benjamin.'

They had no choice but to obey. When they told their father, Jacob, that they had to take Benjamin to Egypt, he wept.

'My darling wife Rachel only had two sons,' he wept. 'Joseph is gone – and now Benjamin too.'

The brothers were upset, too: after all, Joseph had only gone because of their wicked deed.

'We will take care of him,' they promised. 'We will never let him be stolen from you.'

They were true to their promise. Joseph saw how much they wanted to protect Benjamin. He knew they must be sorry for the wrong things they had done so long ago. He knew it was time to forgive and forget.

He burst into tears. 'I am your brother Joseph,' he said. 'God kept me safe in Egypt so I could help you all now.

'Go and fetch my father and everyone in the household. Come to Egypt. We will be a family again.'

Everyone was astonished and delighted all at once. The whole family came to Egypt. Jacob was overjoyed to see his long-lost son.

'May God bless you all,' he said.

The Egyptians

Egypt was the land in which, according to the Bible, the people of Israel lived for hundreds of years – from the time of Joseph to the time of Moses. At first they were welcome, but later they became slaves of the country's ruler – the pharaoh. Moses led their escape.

Egypt's wealth was linked to the River Nile. It flooded each year, spreading silt over the valley. This moist soil was excellent for growing crops.

Gathering papyrus. Thin strips of the stems are used to make paper.

SLAVES ON THE
BUILDING SITE

Making bricks from
a mixture of mud
and chopped straw.

The people of Israel
were forced to work on
grand building projects.

Harvesting the grain.

Recording the crop.

Taking straw to the
basket-makers.

Gathering melons
and cucumbers.

Miriam and her brother

Exodus 1–2

Little Miriam sat beside her mother. She wanted to have a closer look at her new baby brother.

'He's lovely,' she sighed. 'We're going to keep him safe and watch him grow, aren't we?'

The mother wiped away a tear.

'I wish we could,' she said. 'When our people first came to this land of Egypt, we were welcome.

'But that was long ago – before even your great-grandmother was born. The king who rules Egypt now is afraid of our people. He wants all our baby boys to be thrown into the river.'

'We won't do that, will we?' pleaded Miriam.

Together they made a plan. The mother took a basket of coiled reed and covered it with tar to make it waterproof.

Then she placed her baby in it and put a lid on top.

Together, Miriam and her mother took the baby down to the river. They hid the basket among the reeds and left it floating in the still water.

Then the mother went away, and Miriam stayed to watch.

It wasn't long before an Egyptian princess came down to the river to bathe.

As she came to the water's edge, she saw the floating basket.

'Whatever is that!' she exclaimed. Then she spoke to her servants. 'Can you fetch it for me, please?'

The women lifted the basket lid.

'A baby!' they cried.

'I can guess what's happened!' said the princess.
'It must be one of the baby boys whom the king
wants to be flung into the river. Well, he's been in
the river, and now I'm going to take him out and
keep him safe.

'I'm going to call him Moses. I shall adopt him
as my son.'

When Miriam heard this, she stepped forward.

'Would you like me to find someone who can take care of him and feed him till he's older?' she asked.

The princess smiled. 'Yes please,' she said.

Miriam went to fetch her mother, and in no time it was all agreed.

Little Moses grew up with his own family until he was old enough to go to the royal palace.

Moses and the king of Egypt

Exodus 2–15

Moses could hardly believe his eyes. So this was
how the magnificent buildings of Egypt were made!

Moses had grown up as a prince in the royal
palace.

He had known all
along that he belonged to
the people who were
known as Hebrews.

He had known they
worked as slaves on
the king's new
buildings.

However, until this
moment, he had not
known how hard they
had to work, nor how
cruelly they were treated.

Then he saw a slave-driver kill one of the slaves. He was so angry, he fought the slave-driver and killed him.

Someone saw him do it. His guilty secret could not stay hidden. Moses decided that the only safe thing for him to do was to run away. Beyond the borders of Egypt, he made his home among a shepherd people.

One day, he took the flocks in search of pasture. In the shadow of Mount Sinai, he saw an amazing sight. Flames were dancing brightly among the branches of a bush… yet not a leaf was burned.

There, in the wild country, God spoke.

'Moses, I have chosen you. You must go back to Egypt. You must tell the king to let my people go free. You must lead them to a land they can call home.'

Moses was astonished. He was also rather afraid.

'I will be with you,' said God, 'and I will give you power to work wonders.

'Listen – throw your stick onto the ground right now.'

Moses did so. At once, the stick turned into a wriggling snake. Moses gasped and leapt away.

'Come back,' laughed God, 'and pick it up by its tail!'

Moses crept back. He looked hard at the snake. Then he made a grab for it.

At once, it became just a stick again.

'You see,' said God. 'With the power that I can give you, people will be sure to believe you.'

Moses frowned. 'I'm not a good talker,' he argued. 'I fall over my words. No one will listen.'

'Very well,' replied God. 'Then ask your brother Aaron to do the talking.'

Moses went to find Aaron, and together they went to the king of Egypt.

'Your Majesty,' they said. 'The people who work as your slaves came to Egypt in the time of a man named Israel. They are all his children.

'They worship one God: the God of Israel. That God has a message for you: let the people go.'

The king frowned a little. 'I've never heard of the God of Israel,' he replied, 'so I see no reason to obey. I need my slaves. You've simply made me think about what an idle bunch they are. I shall have to put that right.'

The king of Egypt did as he said. He made the people of Israel work harder than ever before.

The slaves were sad and angry. 'You've made everything worse,' they complained to Moses. 'We've always had to make bricks for the king – and it's very hard work. Now we have to fetch our own brick-making stuff as well. Why did you start all this nonsense about leaving?'

Moses and Aaron felt very downcast, and they poured out their troubles to God.

'Be patient,' said God. 'The king hasn't seen what I can do yet.'

Because the king would not listen, all kinds of things began to go wrong in Egypt.

First, the water in the great River Nile turned red and began to stink.

Then the land was overrun with slippery, slimy frogs.

Then great clouds of gnats appeared, and after that, swarms of flies.

The farm animals fell ill. The people fell ill. Hailstorms flattened the crops.

Millions of locusts flew in from the desert and stripped the land of every green and growing thing.

Then all of Egypt seemed to fall under a great dark cloud.

In spite of so many disasters, the king would not let the people of Israel go free.

God came and spoke to Moses. 'Listen: on the day

that I tell you, all of the people of Israel must be ready to travel. They must make bread without yeast that day so they don't have to wait for it to rise. They must kill a lamb for supper and mark their houses with its blood. This mark will show that they are my people.

'Disaster will not strike any house that bears the mark, but pass over it. My people will remember this for ever as Passover night.

'In the homes of the Egyptians, death will strike the firstborn. Then, at last, they will know for sure that I am God. They will plead with you to take my people far away.'

And so it was. The grieving Egyptians came hurrying with gifts for the people of Israel. 'Take our gold, take our silver – just go away and leave us in peace,' they begged.

The people of Israel were dressed and ready. Even their uncooked bread dough was neatly tucked into pans.

'Come on,' they urged one another. 'We can't trust the king of Egypt. We must get far away – and quickly!'

They had not gone many miles when they heard the sound of chariots thundering towards them. It was the Egyptian army, coming to capture them all.

98

'Help!' cried the people. 'Where can we go? The army is driving us towards the Red Sea.'

Then God spoke to Moses. 'Lift up your stick,' said God. 'When you do, I will send a strong east wind to open a way through the sea. You will lead the people through.

'The Egyptians will not be able to follow.'

By a miracle, the people of Israel walked safely through the sea. They could not have been happier. The women danced and played tambourines. Everyone joined with Moses in noisy songs of thanksgiving.

God and God's people

Exodus 16, 19–20, 24–26, 40

The people of Israel believed with all their heart that God had chosen the land of Canaan to be their home.

But between Egypt and Canaan lay the wild country, where they lived as nomads for forty years.

In that time, they found out more about God's love and care.

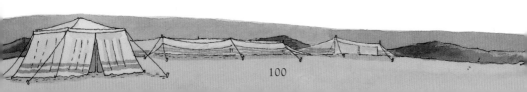

It was God who helped them to find pure water to drink.

It was God who sent flocks of quails that they could eat.

It was God who sent the sweet dew that dried in the early morning sun to leave thin white flakes that were good to eat: food from heaven that the people called manna.

One day, Moses climbed up the tall and mysterious Mount Sinai. There, he heard God speaking to him, and when he came down, he had important things to say.

'God is our holy God,' he said. 'This is what we must do to live as God's holy people. Listen to God's laws and obey them:

'One: Worship God and God alone.

'Two: Do not let anything else be as important to you as God.

'Three: Do not use the name of God in the wrong way.

'Four: Every seventh day is to be God's holy day, a sabbath day of rest for you and all your household.

'Five: Respect your mother and your father.

'Six: Do not murder.

'Seven: Husbands and wives, be faithful to each other.

'Eight: Do not steal.

'Nine: Do not tell lies to get someone into trouble.

'Ten: Do not be greedy for what other people have.'

The ten great laws that Moses brought the people from God were carved onto tablets of stone.

Even the little children could learn them, counting them on their fingers.

'There is more to tell you,' said Moses. 'We must build a special place to remind us that God lives among us. I will choose priests to lead our worship.

'Bring your finest materials for the work: gold and silver; bronze and jewels; acacia wood and leather; smooth white linen and rich woollen fabric in red and blue and purple.

'As we are nomads, our place of worship will be a tent – a tabernacle.

'For its innermost room we will make a beautiful golden box, and in the box we will put the stone tablets that tell us the ten great laws.

'The box will be the symbol of our agreement with God – our covenant to live as God's people.'

When all the work was done, the people gathered round the tent of worship. All at once it seemed to be filled with light.

Everyone believed that this was a sign to show that God was with them.

The tent of worship

In the time of Moses, the people were nomads living in tents. They even made a tent of worship, called the tabernacle. Everyone brought materials for the project.

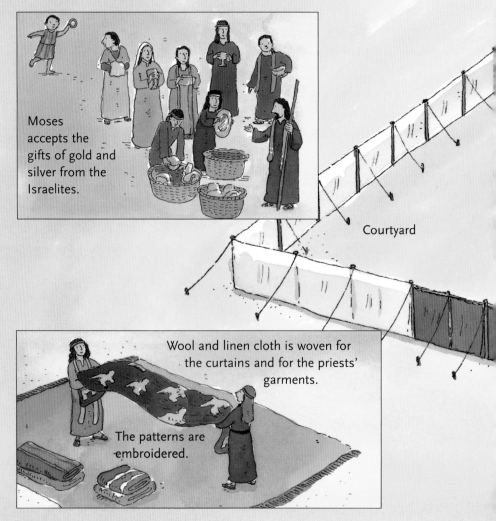

Moses accepts the gifts of gold and silver from the Israelites.

Courtyard

Wool and linen cloth is woven for the curtains and for the priests' garments.

The patterns are embroidered.

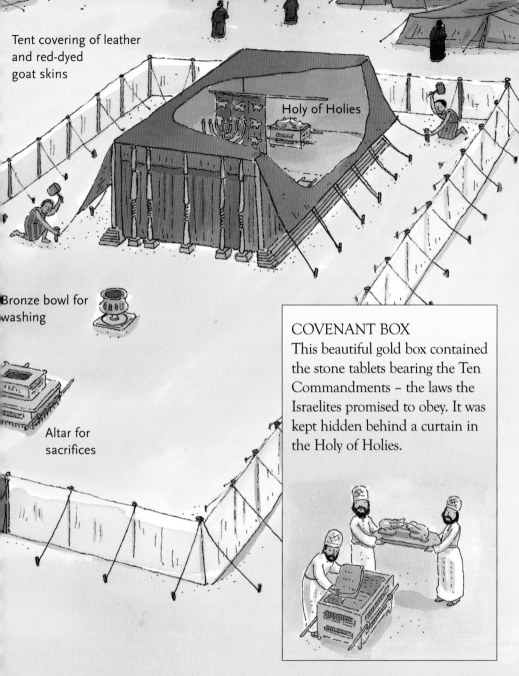

Tent covering of leather and red-dyed goat skins

Holy of Holies

Bronze bowl for washing

Altar for sacrifices

COVENANT BOX

This beautiful gold box contained the stone tablets bearing the Ten Commandments – the laws the Israelites promised to obey. It was kept hidden behind a curtain in the Holy of Holies.

Brave Joshua

Joshua 1, 3, 6, 13, 23–24

When Moses grew old, he chose a younger man to lead the people. Only then could he die in peace.

Moses' choice was Joshua – a fighter who had shown himself to be both brave and wise.

Joshua was also eager to obey God and ready to listen to whatever God had to say to him.

'The time has come,' God told him. 'I promised Moses that I would let my people make their home in the land of Canaan. Now that promise is going to come true.

'Be confident. Be determined. Obey my laws. I will be with you and I will help you in all you do.'

Joshua trusted God. Boldly he led all the people down to the River Jordan. All they had to do was cross it, and they would be in Canaan.

'But surely that's dangerous!' exclaimed the people. 'The river is in flood. Look at how much water is coming down.'

'God has told me what to do,' explained Joshua. 'The priests are to walk into the water carrying the golden covenant box. Then everyone will cross after them.'

When the priests stepped into the river, the water slowed to a trickle. Everyone hurried across.

As the priests stepped out behind them on the other side, the water came roaring down.

Joshua led the people to a place outside the city of Jericho. It was a fortress town built inside strong walls. The city gates were firmly shut. Guards peered down from the walls.

God spoke to Joshua. 'I will give you this city. You and your soldiers are to march round it once a day for six days.

'Priests must carry the golden covenant box as part of the procession. Ahead of them will go seven other priests, each carrying a trumpet.'

Joshua obeyed. For six days in a row the guards on the walls of Jericho watched and wondered.

'On the seventh day,' said God, 'you and your soldiers are to march round the city seven times while the priests blow their trumpets.

'Then the priests are to sound one long note. When you hear it, all the people must shout as loud as they can.'

When they did so, the walls of Jericho collapsed. The soldiers rushed inside and captured the city.

It was a great victory for Joshua. More than that, it was only the first of many victories up and down the land of Canaan.

By the time Joshua was old, the people of Israel had won a great deal of land.

God spoke to Joshua. 'It is time for you to make sure that everyone has a place to call home. All the people can trace their family line back to one of the sons of Israel. You must give a piece of land to each great family.'

So began a time of peace. The people of Israel were able to plough the land and sow seeds. They were able to gather crops and celebrate the harvest.

They were free, as God had promised.

Then Joshua called the people together one last time.

He told them, 'We all know the stories of our people from long ago. They show us how God has kept us safe through the years. Now, we believe, God has blessed us by giving us this land to live in.

'The people who live round about us worship other gods. You must choose whom to worship: the God of our people or those other gods.

'As for me and my family, we will serve the God of Israel.'

All the people shouted joyfully together. 'We will worship our God! We will keep God's laws.'

All God's blessings were theirs to enjoy.

Peoples of Canaan

Joshua led the people of Israel to Canaan – the land they believed
God had promised them in the time of Abraham. Other peoples
already lived there, and there were many battles.

CANAANITES

The Canaanites lived in city states
such as Jericho.

The farmland is
outside the city.

Traders take oil
and wine to the
nearest port.

Stone altar on a 'high place'
where sacrifices are offered
to the Canaanite god Baal,
lord of the weather.

PHILISTINES

The Philistines had invaded Canaan from their home across the sea. They lived on the coast and made frequent attempts to conquer more land. By the time of Samuel, they were famous for having mastered the skill of making iron weapons, which were much stronger than the old bronze weapons.

MIDIANITES
These desert raiders were greatly feared.

Daring Deborah

Judges 4

Deborah sat in the shade of a palm tree and watched the people going by.

She frowned as she saw just how many were taking one particular path.

'Off to worship at those not-so-secret shrines,' she grumbled to herself. 'It's no wonder we've been defeated by a Canaanite king when everyone is so keen to worship the Canaanite gods.'

Then she saw someone else coming up the road: Barak, the soldier she had asked to come and visit her and a man truly devoted to the God of Israel. He came and sat in the shade with her.

'Thank you for coming,' she said. 'The reason I sent for you is of the greatest importance. God has told me the time is right for us to break free from that cruel King Jabin. It is you who must lead an army of 10,000 men against him. You will fight on the plain by the River Kishon.'

Barak's eyes opened wide, and Deborah saw he was afraid.

'Jabin has a very strong army, you know. He even has a chariot regiment: that's 900 iron fighting machines.'

'Are you saying you won't go?' Deborah sounded fierce as she glared at Barak.

'I'll go if you come too,' he mumbled.

Barak gathered an army of volunteers and went to do battle against the Canaanite king.

Deborah stood by his side, smiling grimly. 'God has promised us that we will win,' she said. 'It is only right that we should be free to live as God's own people.'

'I hope you're right,' replied Barak. 'Look: the king has put his commander Sisera in charge. You can see his chariot glittering in the sunlight over there.'

'You must lure him into battle on this flat land by the river,' said Deborah. 'And don't expect the day to stay sunny.'

As the armies lined up to fight, the sky grew dark with clouds. 'Charge!' cried Sisera… and as he did so, thunder rolled across the sky.

Then the rain came in torrents. The iron chariot wheels churned the earth to mud… and sank deeper and deeper.

'Now,' said Deborah to Barak. 'Now you go and claim the victory.'

The Israelites won the day. It was the beginning of an era of freedom and peace for them.

Gideon and the desert raiders

Judges 6–7

Gideon lifted his flail and beat the harvested wheat. Threshing was always hard work and it was going to take a long time for him to do the job alone, especially as he was trying to keep his activity secret.

At least he was strong. And being angry made him feel even stronger.

He was angry about the hated Midianites. The land of Israel was overrun with them. They rode in on camels and stole whatever cattle, sheep and goats they wanted. They destroyed any crops that were growing.

He was lucky to have a harvest at all.

Then he heard a noise.

Someone had crept up behind him.

'God is with you,' said the stranger.

'Oh really?' replied Gideon. 'I hadn't noticed. God hasn't exactly kept the raiders away.'

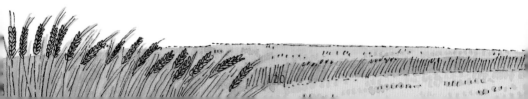

In his heart, he knew why. The people of Israel had
turned away from worshipping God. They did not
live as God's people should. It made them easy prey.

The stranger spoke again: 'God has chosen you.
God wants you to use your great strength to rescue
the people of Israel.'

Gideon was astonished. 'I don't know that I believe
you,' he said.

'I will give you the proof you need,' came the reply.

The mysterious stranger conjured up fire – and vanished.

'That was God's angel,' whispered Gideon. 'I must do what God wants.'

He gathered a huge army: more than 30,000 fighters got ready to follow him into battle.

Then Gideon's courage failed. 'Please God,' he prayed, 'I need proof that I'm doing the right thing. Look, I'll put this bundle of wool on the ground overnight. If you want me to fight, put dew on the wool and leave the ground dry.'

In the morning, that was what he found.

'Oh dear,' he fretted. 'I'm still not sure. Please God… if I put the wool out a second time, will you make the wool dry and the ground wet?'

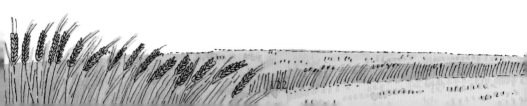

God gave Gideon the sign he needed. After that, he set off with his army.

'You have too many soldiers,' whispered God. 'Not all of them are brave. Say that anyone who wishes to can go home.'

Over 20,000 men breathed a sigh of relief and went.

'Now,' said God, 'take the 10,000 fighters down to the river to drink. Many will kneel. They don't understand that danger lurks. Keep only those who stay standing and scoop up handfuls of water.'

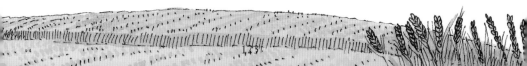

Gideon was left with just 300 fighting men.

The enemy army had many thousands.

'Don't worry,' said God to Gideon. 'To begin with, just go with one man to spy on the camp.'

Gideon went down from the hilltop to the camp on the plain. He was so close he could hear two soldiers talking.

'I had a scary dream,' said one. 'A giant loaf of bread rolled into our camp and flattened a tent.'

'Oh dear!' replied his companion. 'Perhaps it means that Gideon will flatten us.'

Gideon raced back to his men, feeling suddenly confident.

'We will ambush the enemy tonight,' he said. 'Everyone must take a trumpet and a lit torch hidden in a jar. When we are close, I will give the signal.

Blow your trumpet, smash the jar, hold the flaming torch high and shout.'

In the dead of night, the enemy awoke to the terrifying noise. Men were shouting: 'My sword is for God and for Gideon.'

In the dark and the confusion, the enemy fought anyone and everyone. In fact, they fought with one another. Then they ran away.

In this way, God and Gideon brought peace to Israel.

At home in Canaan

When the people of Israel settled in Canaan, they built simple houses for themselves.

A PILLARED HOUSE

Flax is left drying in the sun, to free the fibres that make linen.

A fig tree is shaped to give shade on the roof.

The roof is useful for storing things.

Animals are sheltered in the courtyard.

A lamp in an alcove

A low table and stools

INSIDE A HOUSE

Beds are rolled away in the daytime.

An ox ploughing the field.

An outside staircase leads to the upper storey.

A vegetable plot

Leeks

Beans

As settlers, the people of Israel could begin to farm the land.

Onions

27

Samson the strong

Judges 13–16

When the people of Israel obeyed God's laws, all was well.

Whenever they turned away from doing what was good and right, troubles came.

One terrible trouble was the Philistines, a warrior people who had come to the land of Canaan from far away over the sea. One day, they left their strong cities by the coast and defeated the people of Israel. They ruled over them for forty years.

Then God's angel came with good news. The angel spoke first to a woman – the wife of a man named Manoah. 'You have been childless for many years,' said the angel, 'but soon you will have a son. You must bring him up to know that his life has been given to God. A sign of this will be his hair: it must never be cut.'

The woman and her husband were amazed at the news; but they were delighted to have a son at last. When the child was born, they named him Samson.

He grew up to be very strong. And he liked to get his own way.

Then he fell in love with a Philistine girl. His mother and father were horrified. 'Why can't you marry a nice girl from our own people?' they pleaded.

But Samson wanted the Philistine girl. They agreed to meet the family.

As Samson and his parents walked to the girl's house, they heard a lion roaring. Samson ran and

killed it with his bare hands. Then he came back as if nothing had happened and they all went on their way.

The wedding date was agreed, and soon Samson had to make the same journey. He went to look at the lion he had killed. Inside, he saw a honeycomb that wild bees had built.

At the wedding, Samson decided to set up a competition for the young Philistine men. 'Here's a riddle,' he said. 'There'll be a prize for all of you if you get it. "Out of the eater, something to eat; out of the strong, something sweet." Go on: see if you can guess what that is!'

The young Philistines hadn't a clue. 'We'll have to ask Samson's bride,' they agreed. 'She'll wheedle the answer out of him. Then she'll tell us and we'll get the prize.'

Their plan worked.

Samson knew he had been cheated. It made him violently angry. He didn't care about his marriage any more. He simply wanted revenge.

First he went and killed thirty Philistines.

After that, he began to wage his own war of terror against the enemies of his people, destroying their crops and defying their warriors. This went on for twenty years.

And then Samson fell in love again. He fell in love with a beautiful Philistine woman named Delilah. The Philistines saw their chance. They went to Delilah in secret. 'Find out what makes him so strong,' they said. 'We need to find a way to overpower him. If you can help us, there'll be lots of money for you.'

Delilah had to use all of her charm to try to prise the secret out of Samson. In the end, he grew weary of her nagging.

'I'm strong because my life has been given to God,' he said. 'The sign of the promise is my long hair. If it were cut, I'd be as weak as anyone else.'

The next time Samson fell asleep, Delilah cut his hair and betrayed him.

The Philistines made Samson their prisoner. They blinded him and threw him into prison. There, he had to work like an ox, driving the heavy millstones to grind grain.

The Philistines decided to celebrate their victory. They set the day for all five of their kings to come to the temple of their god Dagon. Thousands of men and women crowded into the building and onto the roof.

Everyone sang noisily. They were looking forward to fun and festivity.

'Let's bring Samson here,' cried someone. 'That will be great entertainment!'

Guards went to fetch him. He shuffled in, his legs in chains. They made him stand between the two great pillars.

Samson bowed his head. His hair fell forward: it had grown long again.

'O God,' he prayed, 'give me strength to get even one last time.'

Then he pushed against the pillars. He pushed and he pushed.

The huge pillars creaked out of position and the temple roof caved in. The building crashed down on all the Philistines.

It was Samson's final victory over the enemies of his people.

Ruth's new family

Ruth 1–4

The hillsides around Bethlehem were parched and dry. The harvest had failed, and there was no food to eat.

That was why Elimelech was leaving. He was taking his wife Naomi and their two sons to the region of Moab.

There, Elimelech died. Naomi's sons each got married in Moab, but both men died young. The three women had to fend for themselves.

Then Naomi heard news from Bethlehem. The harvest that year promised to be abundant. She decided that all three of them should go back to her old home.

On the way, she changed her mind.

'I'm sorry,' she said to the younger women. 'You'd be better staying among your own people. You will be able to marry again.'

Both the daughters-in-law burst into tears. 'I don't want to say goodbye,' said one, her voice trembling with sadness, 'but I think you're right.'

She kissed Naomi goodbye.

'I won't leave you,' sobbed the other, whose name was Ruth. 'Your people will be my people. Your God will be my God.'

She wept and pleaded. In the end, Naomi agreed they would travel on together.

Ruth and Naomi arrived in Bethlehem just as the barley harvest was beginning.

'I can go gleaning for grain in the fields,' said Ruth. 'The poor are allowed to take what gets left behind, aren't they?'

Naomi agreed, and the next day Ruth was out in the fields at daybreak.

She was careful to ask permission before she took any of the stalks that the harvesters had left, and she worked very hard to gather all she could.

Later in the day, the owner of the field arrived. His name was Boaz.

'Who is that young woman?' he asked the workers.

'She's the foreigner who came here with Naomi,' came the reply. 'She's been here all day.'

Boaz had already heard about Ruth. He knew that she had been very kind to Naomi.

He went and spoke to her. 'May God bless you!' he said. 'Please stay in this field and gather all the barley you can.'

He then told his workers to leave extra for her to gather.

Boaz made sure that Ruth was able to gather enough to live on all through the barley harvest and the wheat harvest as well.

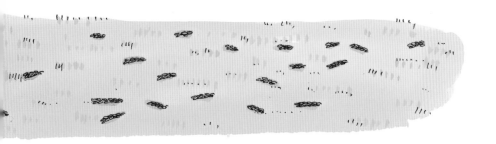

Sometime later, Naomi had an idea. 'Ruth,' she said,
'I think it's time we found a husband for you, so you
will have a home of your own.

'I think that Boaz would be a good choice. He
probably doesn't think you'd want to marry him: he

is rather older than you.

'But I think I know a clever way for you to ask him to marry you.'

The plan worked, and Boaz was delighted that Ruth really did want to marry him.

It wasn't long before everyone in Bethlehem heard the news, and they agreed it was the perfect match.

Ruth and Boaz got married and soon they were the proud parents of a little boy.

Naomi was thrilled to be a grandmother.

God had blessed them all.

Weddings

Weddings in Bible times were usually arranged by the families. A boy and girl might be promised in marriage when they were quite young. The wedding would normally happen when they came of age. A bride and groom would often be aged between thirteen and fourteen.

The bride's attendants light the way with their lamps.

The bridegroom's friends carry him in a great procession to his bride.

During the festivities, the bride and groom sat under a canopy. Everyone expected a feast.

Wine

Roasted calf

Honey cakes

Music and dancing

Samuel hears a call

1 Samuel 1–4, 6–7

When the people of Israel made their home in Canaan, they chose Shiloh to be the place of worship. People used to go there for special festivals.

There came a time when a priest named Eli was in charge there. For many years he had done his best to help the people worship God faithfully. Now he was getting old, and he was glad to have two sons to help him.

One day, he was sitting by the place of worship when he saw a woman who had come for the festival. She was acting oddly.

'I think you're drunk!' said Eli angrily. 'Go away till you're fit to worship!'

'I'm sorry,' wept the woman, 'but I'm not drunk. I'm simply very unhappy because I have no children. I was asking God to let me have a son.'

'Oh,' said Eli, rather more gently. 'Well, may God bless you.'

A few years later, the woman came to a festival at Shiloh again. She rushed up to Eli. 'Do you remember me?' she asked. 'I'm Hannah, and I'm the one you thought was drunk.

'God really did bless me. See – I wanted a son and here he is. I want to give him back to God. Will you take my little Samuel as your helper here?'

Eli was delighted. He took care of the boy and told him all he needed to know to be a useful helper.

Every year, Hannah came to Shiloh and she always brought a new tunic she had made for her son.

She was so pleased to see him growing up. Samuel was faithful to God and faithful to Eli.

In fact, he was much more faithful than Eli's sons.

One night, Samuel was taking his turn to sleep in the place of worship, where the golden covenant box was kept. It was his job to make sure the lamps had enough oil to keep on burning.

He heard someone calling him by name. It must be Eli, he thought. Things are different for him now that he is going blind.

He hurried to the room where Eli was in bed.

'Here I am!' he said brightly.

'Why?' asked Eli. 'I didn't call you.'

'Oh, sorry,' said Samuel, and he went back to the place of worship.

All of a sudden, he again heard someone calling his name. Once again, he hurried off to see Eli.

But Eli hadn't called him, and he sent him back again.

A third time, Samuel heard someone calling.

He went to Eli. 'You did call,' he said, 'and here I am.'

Then Eli understood. 'It must be God speaking,' he explained. 'If you hear the call again, you must tell God you are listening.'

In the morning, Eli asked Samuel if God had truly spoken to him, and what God had said.

Samuel hung his head. He was afraid to explain. 'God told me that your sons are not going to be priests after you,' he said. 'They have not been faithful to God.'

Eli was sad, but he understood.

Even so, he didn't expect what happened next. The people of Israel were going to war against the Philistines, and they wanted to have the covenant box with them. Eli's sons took it to the battlefield. There they were killed, and the covenant box was captured.

Eli died of sorrow.

All the people of Israel were dismayed. They were afraid that God had turned away from them.

But God had a new plan for the people. When, at last, the enemy realized that the covenant box only seemed to bring them one disaster after another, they sent it back. By then Samuel was ready to be a wise leader of his people.

He helped them to worship God faithfully. He helped them to understand the laws. He helped people to live in the way that was good and right, and be friends with one another.

Prophets and priests

The people of Israel had rules about how to choose their priests. Prophets, however, felt they were called directly by God. They told the people what they believed God was saying to them.

The Bible tells us how the prophet Moses went up Mount Sinai and returned with the laws God had spoken to him.

Elijah was a prophet who warned wicked King Ahab to be faithful to God.

PRIESTS

Priests were those in charge of Israel's place of worship and the ceremonies there. The twelve stones on the high priest's breastplate and the twelve loaves set out as an offering were a reminder of the twelve tribes of Israel.

The high priest burns incense in front of the Holy of Holies.

Helper

The lamps on the seven-branched lampstand – the menorah – are always kept burning in the place of worship.

Priest

Choosing a king

1 Samuel 8–10, 15–16

The people of Israel were worried, and they went to tell Samuel exactly what was worrying them.

'You're getting older,' they reminded him, 'but your sons are not wise like you. We want you to choose someone to be a king. All the other peoples have a king: someone who can lead them into war and help them win.'

Samuel was very upset, and complained to God. 'The people have rejected me,' he said.

'Don't worry,' said God. 'Really it's me they don't trust. But anyway, I will help you find the right person.'

Not long after, Samuel met a young man named Saul. He was tall and strong.

'This is the new king,' whispered God. 'Now you must make him king in front of everyone.'

As soon as he could, Samuel called all the people together. Together, they went through a long ceremony of choosing.

It was quite clear: Saul was the man God had chosen to be king.

'Long live the king,' cheered the people.

Soon Saul was leading his people into battle.

He and his army won great victories.

However, as the years went by, he stopped listening to Samuel's advice about how to treat his enemies.

He stopped listening to Samuel's advice about what to do with the things he captured.

'I'm sorry,' said God to Samuel. 'We're going to have to choose again.

'I want you to go to Bethlehem. There you will find a man named Jesse. He has many fine sons. I will show you which one is to be king.'

Samuel went, and Jesse introduced his eldest son. He was tall and strong. 'It's not him!' Samuel heard God say. 'I don't care what people look like. It's who they are inside that matters.'

One by one, Samuel met seven sons. He was puzzled. Every time, God whispered no.

'Don't you have any more sons?' asked Samuel.

'Only the youngest,' said Jesse. 'He's out looking after the sheep. I'll send for him.'

Jesse's youngest son David came up the hill, humming tunefully.

He greeted Samuel with a cheerful smile, and as he did so his eyes sparkled.

'This is the next king,' whispered God to Samuel.

There and then, Samuel performed the king-making ceremony: he poured olive oil over the young man's head.

David danced and sang for joy: he knew that God was truly with him.

Then he went back to his sheep. For the moment, Saul was still king and he was still a shepherd boy with hours to spend on the hillside, watching the sheep, playing his harp and practising his aim with the slingshot.

Samuel sighed. He might never live to see the young man become king; but he felt sure that Israel's future was safe.

Warriors

Throughout Bible history, the people of Israel needed a fighting force. War was part of Joshua's campaign to make Canaan a land that his people could settle in. Strong leaders such as Deborah and Gideon led soldiers against the tribes that threatened them. Each time, fighters had to be 'called up'.

King Saul was the first leader to set up a permanent army, and King David and King Solomon after him made it stronger. However, the Israelites never had an army to match those of the great empires.

SAUL'S ARMY
When he was first king, Saul had to summon an army. He sent messengers with trumpets to every community.

Saul's army had only foot soldiers. They probably had to bring their own weapons: swords, bows and arrows, and slings.

KING SOLOMON'S ARMY
King Solomon ruled a wealthy nation. At last the army could have cavalry and chariot regiments.

A slingshot was not just for shepherds. It was an army weapon. There were even 'regiments' of slingers.

David and Goliath

1 Samuel 17–31; 2 Samuel 1–5; Psalm 23

King Saul's army lined up on the hillside, ready for battle.

On the hillside across the valley was the enemy army: the Philistines, whose strong iron weapons glinted in the sunshine.

The Israelite soldiers looked at one another. 'Only the king and his son have swords that are as strong as those,' they whispered.

As they waited, two men came striding out of the

enemy camp. One wore heavy bronze armour and a bronze helmet. The other was smaller, a boy perhaps, carrying the shield.

'The tall one's wearing more metal than we've got in our weapons,' muttered an Israelite. 'I hope I don't meet him in battle.'

The taller man shouted across the valley. His voice was harsh and mocking.

'Who dares fight me?' he roared. 'I am Goliath, the champion warrior of the Philistines. Beat me in single combat and you win the war. Lose, and you'll be our slaves!'

He brandished his huge spear, and all the Israelites cowered. No one dared fight him.

Every day for forty days, Goliath roared his challenge and laughed his mocking laugh. The Israelites grew more and more afraid.

One day, the shepherd boy named David arrived at the Israelite camp. His elder brothers were in Saul's army and he had brought food from home to give them.

He heard the challenge.

He heard about the big reward that was on offer for anyone who beat Goliath.

'I'd love to try!' he told everyone.

King Saul heard the news that someone had volunteered to try to win the war. He demanded to see whoever it was.

As the young man was led towards him, Saul stood up eagerly. Then he sank back down. 'Oh no!' he said. 'You're a boy – you'd never last against Goliath. He's been a soldier all his life.'

'Your Majesty,' replied David. 'I'm a shepherd boy. I've killed lions and bears who tried to steal the lambs. I can do the same to this Philistine. God has kept me safe from wild animals; God will keep me safe from this Philistine.'

Saul glowered at him. 'Well, you're the only one to offer,' he said sulkily. 'But give yourself a chance: at least take my armour.'

David was eager to try it on and to hold the precious iron sword; but he could hardly move, let alone fight.

'I'll just go with what I'm used to,' he said cheerfully.

David set off across the valley with just his shepherd's stick and a slingshot. He stopped by the brook to pick five smooth stones. Then he went to face Goliath.

'How dare you!' shouted Goliath. 'A stick's only good to beat a dog. And you're only fit for the wild animals to eat.'

'You've got a sword, a spear and a javelin,' said David. 'I'm fighting in the name of my powerful God.'

Goliath strode towards David, but David ran to meet him. He took a stone, whirled it in his slingshot, and sent it spinning towards the warrior.

It hit right on target. Goliath fell forward. Before he could stand up, David had taken his sword and killed him.

The Philistines fled in terror. David became the Israelites' hero.

King Saul was delighted to have won the war, but he was not so pleased about how popular David was.

David always tried to please him. Time and again he showed that he was a brave and loyal fighter.

With each success, Saul grew more and more jealous. In the end, David had to run away and live as an outlaw. Saul tried to hunt him down, but David was too clever for him.

Many people in Israel still thought of David as a hero. Soon he had his own band of fighting men. They lived dangerously, never knowing who was truly a friend and who was an enemy.

The day came when Saul was killed in a battle against the Philistines.

'Now is the time,' said David to his supporters. 'I will be your king. With your help, I will one day be king over all the people of Israel.'

It took a long time to win everyone's trust, but David was confident.

At last he triumphed.

David built himself a royal city on a hilltop: the city of Jerusalem.

He longed to build a splendid temple there, where all the people of Israel could come to worship. To get ready for that day, he set up a beautiful tent like the one that had been made in the time of Moses. He arranged for the covenant box to be brought there in a noisy and joyful parade.

In time, he defeated all his enemies. As he looked back over everything that had happened, he knew for sure that God had been taking care of him, as he had been when he was a shepherd boy.

He had always enjoyed singing and playing the harp. Now he was able to write beautiful songs.

The Lord God is my shepherd,
   and I am God's own sheep;
God takes me to green pastures
   and water clear and deep.
When enemies come near me,
   and fear is all around,
The Lord God will defend me:
   I stand on holy ground.
God spreads a feast before me
   and everyone can see
The goodness and the kindness
   the Lord God shows to me.

Wise King Solomon

1 Kings 2–3, 5–6, 8, 10

When David died, his son Solomon became king.
He was only a young man, and he was anxious to
do everything right.

One night, God spoke to him in a dream.

'What would you like me to give you?' asked God.

Solomon was ready with his answer. 'Please make me wise, so I can rule your people well.'

'That is a very good answer,' replied God. 'I will give you more wisdom than anyone.

'I will also give you the things that so many kings want: you will have enormous wealth, and you will be respected by everyone, both near and far.'

When Solomon woke up, he knew exactly what to do first.

He went to the beautiful tent in Jerusalem where the covenant box was kept. In a special ceremony, he gave thanks to God and God alone.

Not long after, Solomon's wisdom was put to the test.

Two women came to see him. They were arguing noisily, and the argument was all about a baby.

'Please listen,' pleaded the first. 'We both had babies within days of each other, but then hers died. This wretch came in the night and stole my child.'

'That's a wicked lie,' cried the second. 'Her child died, and the lovely baby here is mine.'

'He is so clearly my own little boy!'

'No he's not! A mother never forgets her baby – not after the first glimpse of its dear sweet face.'

Solomon listened, his gaze switching from one woman to the other.

He nodded to a servant. 'Fetch a sword,' he said.

When the sword was brought, he gave it to the guard who was holding the baby. 'Cut the child in half,' he said. 'They can have half each.'

'NO!' screamed the first. 'Give him to her! Don't hurt the baby. She can have him.'

'Yes, I will have him,' said the second, and she reached out her arms.

'Give the baby to the first woman,' said Solomon. 'I know she is the mother, for she will do anything to save her child.'

Solomon also knew it was wise to build a temple – the temple that his father David had wanted to build. A temple that would make everyone in the kingdom proud to be one of God's people.

Under his rule, the kingdom had grown wealthy, and Solomon was able to order the finest materials: stone and timber from far away, and vast amounts of bronze and gold.

The craftworkers gave the project all their skill and love.

At last, the finished Temple stood gleaming on the hilltop, and the covenant box was placed in the innermost room.

All the people came to see, and to renew their promise to be faithful to God and God's laws.

News of Solomon's wealth and wisdom spread far and wide. The queen of Sheba came on a lavish state visit, bringing rich gifts of spices, jewels and pure gold.

She asked Solomon many questions and was amazed at his clever answers.

'Now I truly understand how much your God must love the people of Israel,' she said. 'God has made you their king so you can rule them with justice.'

Never before had the people of Israel been so united and strong.

Solomon's golden Temple

In the time of King Solomon, the people of Israel had wealth and peace. King Solomon's father, King David, had made an ancient hilltop fort into his royal city, Jerusalem. Solomon built a temple in Jerusalem. It followed the design of the tabernacle. The Temple lasted until the time the Babylonians came and destroyed the city.

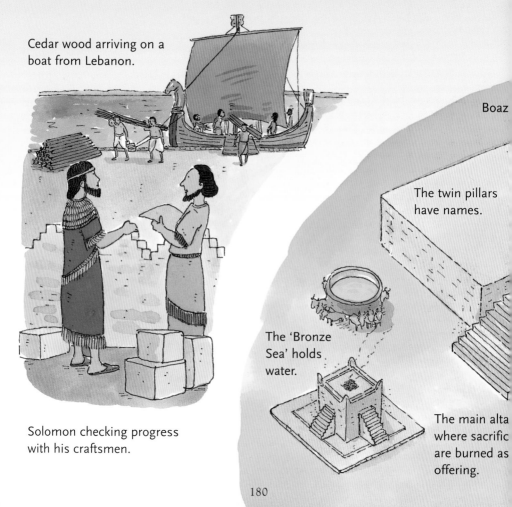

Cedar wood arriving on a boat from Lebanon.

Boaz

The twin pillars have names.

The 'Bronze Sea' holds water.

Solomon checking progress with his craftsmen.

The main alta where sacrific are burned as offering.

The outside walls are stone.
The inside walls are
covered in gold.

The covenant box in
the Holy of Holies

Table

Menorah

Incense altar

Jachin

Storerooms

Bronze carts

Elijah and the king

1 Kings 17–18

Elijah sat down by the river and sighed. Everything had gone wrong.

The people of Israel were in turmoil. It was hard to believe they had ever gathered as one nation to worship God at Solomon's golden Temple. Now they were divided: a kingdom in the south and a kingdom in the north.

In the northern kingdom, Ahab was the king. He had no respect for the God of his people; instead, he worshipped a foreign god, Baal.

Elijah was a prophet, and his job was to help people live as God's people should. Ahab never listened. That was certain to lead to trouble.

'I'm in charge of the weather,' God had told Elijah, 'and I'm not going to send any rain for a very long time. However, I am going to keep you safe, Elijah.

Go to the Cherith brook and stay there.'

So that's where Elijah was. He watched the water trickling over the pebbles; then he looked around and found a place where he could shelter for as long as he needed to.

For many days he was able to drink from the brook. By a miracle, ravens brought him all the food he needed.

Then the brook dried up.

'I will tell you where to go,' said God to Elijah. 'On your way, you will meet a woman gathering firewood. She will be able to take care of you.'

Elijah went where he was told, and in time he met the woman just as God had said.

'Please can you give me water to drink and a meal to eat?' he asked.

'I'm sorry,' replied the woman. 'There has been no rain, so there's no harvest and no food. All I have left is a handful of flour and a drop of oil in a jar. It will only make one small meal for me and my son.'

'Don't worry,' said Elijah. 'Make the meal you need; but when you do, make a small loaf for me too. God is making a promise: there will always be flour in the bowl and oil in the jar.'

The woman agreed to do as Elijah said. By a miracle,

they had food through the three long years when no
rain fell.

Then God spoke to Elijah again. 'It's time to go
and talk to King Ahab. It's time he learned the
difference between worshipping Baal and worshipping
me. We will have a contest.'

Elijah listened to God's plan. Then, feeling rather
afraid, he went and told Ahab.

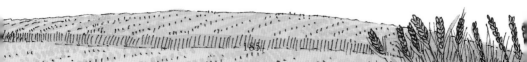

The king didn't want to have a contest, but he did want rain. Angrily, he agreed to Elijah's plan.

On the chosen day, he came to meet Elijah on the top of a high mountain. With him came 450 prophets who worshipped Baal.

All the people in Ahab's kingdom came to watch.

'Today, we are going to find out who is really in charge of everything,' said Elijah. 'Is it God, or is it Baal?

'The prophets of Baal must first build a pile of firewood. Then they must put a gift of food on top. Then they must ask Baal to take it by setting it all on fire. After that, I'll do the same for God.'

The prophets of Baal set to work. They brought heaps of wood which was dry and ready for

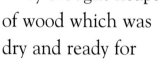

burning. After that, they laid the food gift on top.

Then they prayed to Baal. 'Fire! Send the fire and take our gift!'

Nothing happened.

'Keep praying,' said Elijah. 'You never know. Maybe Baal is daydreaming. Maybe he's gone to the toilet. Maybe he's having a little walk or something.'

The prophets prayed louder. They got into a complete frenzy. Nothing happened.

After many hours, Elijah
stood up. 'It's time to see what
God can do,' he said.

'Everyone come close and watch.
Look, this pile of stones used to be an altar
where we came to offer gifts to God. I'm going
to repair it. Then I'll pile up the firewood and lay
the food gift on top.'

Elijah did as he said. He also dug a ditch around
the altar.

'Now I want people to pour lots of water
over this,' he said.

The water soaked the wood and
made a puddle in the ditch.

'More water please,' said Elijah.
'I want it really wet.'

When the altar was drenched,
Elijah prayed aloud.

'O God, please show everyone
that you are the true God of Israel.'

The heap of wood burst into flames. Tongues of fire ate the wood and gift of food, and they licked the water dry.

'The God of Israel is truly our God!' shouted the people.

'Then it's time to get rid of everything to do with Baal,' said Elijah. 'Soon, the God of Israel will send rain.'

Elijah smiled. God's power had been shown to everyone.

King Hezekiah's enemies

2 Kings 18–19

The people of Israel never stayed faithful to God alone for long. In his palace in Jerusalem, King Hezekiah bowed his head as he recalled their history.

He remembered the stories of long ago, when the

people of Israel had settled in the land and made it their home.

Then, they had promised to obey God and to be God's people.

In the kingdom to the north, the people had not been faithful. Their last chance was over.

An enemy army had come marching in from the great city of Nineveh. It had beaten them utterly and sent them to faraway places.

'And now the enemy is here, in my tiny kingdom,' sighed Hezekiah. 'Those terrifying Assyrians! They're capturing it bit by bit – even though I've been as faithful to God as I possibly can be.

'Well, there's only one way out: I'll take the gold and silver from the Temple that they are demanding and give it to them in return for peace.'

Hezekiah sent the gold and silver, but the enemy did not want peace.

They marched closer to Jerusalem and set up camp all around.

They sent messengers with a warning. They shouted to the people who watched in fear from the city walls. 'Listen, everyone in Jerusalem. Don't be foolish: Hezekiah can't save you, and neither can his God.

'Give in now. We can offer you a new life in one of the many wonderful places that our emperor rules.'

The people of Jerusalem looked down, but they didn't answer. Three of the king's trusted officials hurried

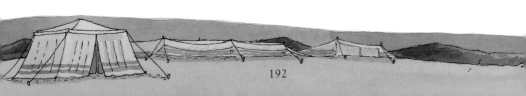

to tell the king what was going on.

Hezekiah wept when he heard the news. 'I'm going to the Temple to pray,' he told his servants. 'Then I want to send a message to Isaiah. He's a true prophet: the advice he gives is from God alone.'

Hezekiah prayed with all his heart. He waited for the servants to bring word from Isaiah: 'You're not to be afraid,' they said. 'God is going to rescue the city.'

That night, a strange illness struck the enemy army. It seemed to come from nowhere: people said it was brought by the angel of death.

When the people of Jerusalem peered out from the city walls at dawn, they saw that the remaining soldiers were packing up and getting ready to go home, all the way to the city of Nineveh.

King Hezekiah was left in peace to rule his little kingdom and to make the city of Jerusalem strong and safe.

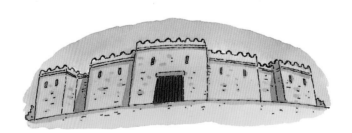

The Assyrians

To the north of Canaan lay Syria and beyond that, Assyria. It was a fertile land that grew good crops, and the Assyrians had time to trade and to go to war and so make themselves wealthy. By the time of the kings of Israel, they had great cities with splendid buildings – including the city of Nineveh, made famous in the story of Jonah.

A ROYAL SCENE

King Ashurbanipal and his queen relax in the palace garden in Nineveh.

ATTACK AT LACHISH

The Assyrians destroyed the northern kingdom of Israel, and attacked the southern kingdom of Judah, winning a victory at the city of Lachish.

Camp

Flaming torches

Siege machines

Prisoners are led away.

The story of Jonah

Jonah 1–4

Once upon a time there lived a man named Jonah.
He was a prophet – so when he gave advice, people
knew that the advice was from God.

One day, God spoke to Jonah. 'Go to the city of
Nineveh. The people there are wicked. I want you to
tell them to change their ways.'

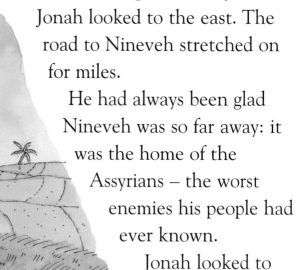

Jonah looked to the east. The
road to Nineveh stretched on
for miles.

He had always been glad
Nineveh was so far away: it
was the home of the
Assyrians – the worst
enemies his people had
ever known.

Jonah looked to

the west. The road led to the sea.

'I think I'll go and take the boat to Spain,' he said.

So off he went to the port of Joppa. He paid his fare and got on the boat, and smiled as he sailed further and further away from the city of Nineveh.

Then he lay down to sleep.

In the night, a storm blew in.

The boat was tossed around on the waves. One moment it was wobbling on a foamy crest, the next it was sliding into a deep, dark trough. Even the sailors were terrified.

'This is a supernatural storm,' they cried. 'Everyone on board, come and help!'

As they struggled to keep the boat afloat, some began to mutter. 'We must play a choosing game to find out which one of us has made their god so angry.'

The choosing game gave them the name they needed: Jonah.

'I'm sorry. It's all my fault,' he wailed. 'I'm running away from God. You'll have to throw me off the boat or we'll all go down to the bottom of the sea.'

The sailors had no choice. 'We're sorry!' they cried, as they hurled him into the water.

As Jonah sank, the sea went calm. Down in the depths, a great fish came and swallowed Jonah whole.

Jonah checked himself all over to make sure he was still alive. He couldn't quite believe what was happening. He was sure of just one thing: he had better learn to obey God. Right away.

'O God,' he prayed, 'you have saved me from death. I will praise you for ever and do what I have promised. O God, you are truly a God who rescues those you love.'

Jonah was used to hearing God speak. However, he was not used to the dreadful rumbling, belching sound all around him. The fish was being sick.

It spat Jonah onto a beach.

'I'll speak now,' said God. 'Jonah, I want you to go to Nineveh and tell the people there to change their wicked ways.'

Jonah hurried to the city as fast as he could.

'Forty days!' he cried. 'God has given you forty days to change your wicked ways. God is angry. God will destroy you all! Nineveh will be no more!'

'Oh no!' cried the people.

'Disaster!' wept the king. 'We must change at once. We must show God we are sorry. Perhaps God will be kind.'

And God was kind.

Jonah was furious. 'So,' he shouted to God, 'now you know why I tried to go to Spain. You're too kind to everyone. Why can't you punish wicked people properly? You make me really cross.'

He trudged out of the city and sat down. Then he decided to make himself a little shelter so he could sit and watch whatever God might do next.

That night, as Jonah slept, God set a little seed growing. It grew and grew, and the plant covered the shelter in large green leaves.

'What lovely shade,' said Jonah. 'I won't mind another hot day now.'

The following night, a worm came. It chewed the juicy green stem, and the plant wilted and died.

Jonah was utterly dismayed. He grew even angrier as the sun came up and the day grew hotter and

hotter. 'My poor, dear plant,' he moaned.

Then he heard God speaking.

'Why worry about the plant?' said God. 'It grew up in one night and died the next. You didn't take any trouble over it... why do you feel sorry for it?'

'My lovely plant!' wailed Jonah.

'So you care about a plant,' said God. 'Do you understand why I feel sorry for the people of Nineveh? I care about those people, and their children, and their animals.'

By the river in Babylon

2 Kings 24–25; 2 Chronicles 36; Psalm 137

The golden Temple in Jerusalem was the pride and joy of all its people. Every time they looked at it, they remembered God. They remembered they were God's people.

They knew the old stories about how God had chosen them and looked after them. They told the stories to their children and their grandchildren… and this went on for years and years.

Then came disaster. In a faraway place named Babylon, a man named Nebuchadnezzar became king.

He led his army to war. He wanted to be king everywhere.

One sad day, he and his army captured Jerusalem. They burnt down the houses and the royal palace.

They stole all the treasure from the Temple. Then they burnt the empty building.

Nebuchadnezzar ordered many of the people to go

and live in Babylon, where he could make sure they obeyed his laws. It was there that the people from Judah were called the Jews.

The Jews were very sad. 'We have no place to worship God,' they wept. 'All we can do is tell the old stories to our children.'

So that is what they did: they met on the banks of the great river of Babylon. There, in the shade of the willow trees, they learned about God and said their prayers.

Daniel and the lions

Daniel 6

Among the people who were taken to Babylon was a man named Daniel. He wanted to stay faithful to God, so every day he turned to look out along the road to Jerusalem and said his prayers.

Daniel also served the kings of Babylon loyally: he was honest and he was wise.

In time, a man named Darius became king, and he chose Daniel to help him rule.

The people who worked alongside him were angry. 'Why has Daniel got the best job? He's even allowed to tell us what to do!'

'We'll have to find a

way to get rid of him.'

'Here's an idea!' said one.

They all huddled together
to listen to the plan.

Then they went to see the
king.

'O King,' they said, 'we
want you to be king for ever.
We want people to respect
you more than any god.

'So we have an idea: you
must make a new law. You
must tell everyone to say
their prayers to you and
you alone.

'Anyone who disobeys must be thrown to the lions.'

'Excellent,' said the king. 'I want absolute
obedience. I'll make the law right now – a law that
can never be changed.'

The men bowed low and then hurried away.

'Let's go and find Daniel,' they said. 'He always prays to God at this time of day. Look! There he is, at the window. What a wicked man he is to break the king's new law.'

They went to tell the king.

'O King,' they said, 'we want you to be king for ever. We want people to respect you more than any god.

'O King, we bring you bad news. That Daniel from Jerusalem still prays to his own God. He isn't obeying your wonderful new law. He must be thrown to the lions.'

The king was not happy. 'I didn't make that law for Daniel,' he said. 'I know I can trust Daniel.'

The men frowned. 'O King,' they said, and they sounded disapproving, 'when you make a law, it can never be changed.

'If you don't punish Daniel, everyone will think they can break the law. No one will respect you. You won't be king for ever.'

'Oh dear,' said the king. 'I suppose you're right. Go and arrest him.'

The king waited at the door of the lion pit. 'I'm sorry,' he said to Daniel. 'I hope your God is as faithful to you as you are to your God.'

Then strong men flung Daniel into the pit and locked the door.

Daniel was all alone with the lions. There was nothing that anyone could do to help him.

In his royal palace, the king paced up and down, up and down. It was night-time, but he couldn't sleep. He didn't want to eat. There was nothing his servants could do to stop him worrying.

The sky was only just turning light when he hurried to the pit.

'Daniel!' called the king. 'Has your God been able to help you?'

'Yes, of course, Your Majesty,' replied Daniel. 'An angel came and stopped the lions from eating me. God knows that I am loyal to you; God knows that I don't deserve to be punished.'

The king ordered Daniel to be lifted to safety.

'Now I know for sure that your God is a great God,' he said.

'I also know exactly who wanted to get Daniel into trouble, and now they're in trouble. It's their turn to go into the pit… and the lions are looking even hungrier than before.'

Babylonians and Persians

East of Assyria lay Babylon, and the time came when the Babylonians defeated the Assyrians. They went on to defeat the people of Judah. Solomon's temple was destroyed and many of the people of Judah were taken to live in Babylon. There they became known as the Jews.

BABYLON

Blue glazed tiles

Mythical beasts

King Nebuchadnezzar had the city of Babylon rebuilt. One of its entrances was called Ishtar Gate after the goddess of love and war.

Processional Way

PERSIA

The Babylonian empire did not last for very long. In less than a century, the Persians had defeated it. They also let the people of Judah go home to Jerusalem and build a new temple. It was not nearly as fine as the great buildings of the Persian cities. The stories of Daniel are set in the time of the Babylonian and Persian empire.

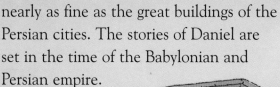

The engraved figures are of Medes and Persians leading defeated nations with their tribute to the emperor.

King Darius admires his new palace at Persepolis.

Nehemiah the builder

Nehemiah 1–12; Zechariah 9

Nehemiah couldn't stop thinking about the news.

There he was, working as a butler for a foreign emperor, Artaxerxes of Persia. He lived in a splendid palace. Meanwhile, some of his fellow Jews had made the long journey back to Jerusalem. They were trying to rebuild the city. Now he had heard that the work was not going well.

He couldn't stop worrying about how to help.

Even the emperor noticed that he was looking sad. 'What's the matter?' he wanted to know, and Nehemiah explained.

'Oh dear,' said the emperor. 'What can I do to help?'

Nehemiah said a silent prayer, asking God to help him answer wisely.

'I'd like to be allowed to go to Jerusalem,' he said. 'It's where my people come from. I'd like to help with the rebuilding.'

'Then you shall go!' said the emperor. 'I will make sure your journey is as easy as possible.'

Soon, Nehemiah was on his way.

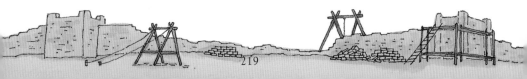

When he reached Jerusalem, he was dismayed at the sight of ruins. He didn't know where to begin rebuilding.

Then, one night, he rode a donkey all the way round the city. What he saw helped him decide on a plan. Soon after, he went and explained it to the people of Jerusalem.

'The city walls are all broken down,' he said. 'I think we should build them new and strong. That will be a sign to everyone that we want to be proud of our city again.'

So the work began. All the Jewish people in the city and round about were eager to be part of the new and exciting plan.

But there was a problem: people from other nations lived close by, and they were jealous of what they saw. They began to whisper together. Nehemiah heard that they were planning to attack. He said a prayer, asking God to help him act wisely.

'We shall have to be ready to fight,' he told the workers. 'At any one time, half of you must stand guard while the others build. I will be on patrol all the time, and a man with a bugle will be with me. If I hear of trouble, he will sound the bugle. At the signal everyone must come and fight.'

The enemy saw that Nehemiah was very determined. They never dared attack.

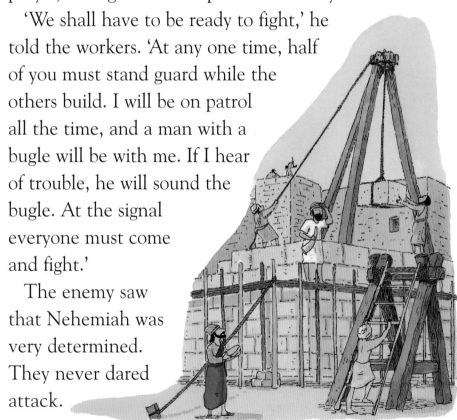

At last the walls were complete. The Jewish people felt safe inside their city. They all met to celebrate.

'God is our God! We want to live as God's people should!' they cried. 'We want Ezra, the priest, to tell us what to do!'

Ezra stood on a wooden platform. He read aloud from the books in which the Law was written, and the people cheered.

The next day Ezra made an announcement. 'Now that I've had a chance to read the Law and think about it,' he said, 'I've just realized that it's time for a special festival. It's time to remember when our people followed Moses through the wild country and had to live in tents. We should spend a week living in rough shelters.'

Everyone was delighted. They went to gather branches from the woods and built little huts and pavilions all through the city.

They celebrated the festival just as their people had done long before. And soon after came another holy

day: the day for everyone to say sorry to God for anything they had done wrong.

'O God,' they prayed, 'we remember all the stories of how you have always looked after our people.

'We give thanks for the way you look after us.

'We are sorry for the times we and all our people have turned away from you.

'We will live as your people for ever.'

Nehemiah was very pleased. As governor of Jerusalem, he did all he could to help the people there live in a way that pleased God.

He did his best to make sure that everyone was treated fairly.

He did his best to make sure that the Temple was put into working order.

He did his best to help people do what was good and right.

In those days, there was a prophet named Zechariah, who brought a message of good news.

'We should all be happy and joyful,' he said. 'God is going to send us a new king. He will come in triumph, but he will come to bring us peace.

'Through him, God will take care of us as a shepherd takes care of his sheep.

'It will be like living in a whole new world, where everything is good and beautiful.'

In between the Testaments

The last stories of the Old Testament are set some 400 years before the stories of Jesus.

In between time, the Greeks became the most powerful people in that part of the world. In their empire everyone spoke Greek, as well as their own language. Greek remained an important language even when the Romans became the new imperial power.

ALEXANDER THE GREAT
Alexander was the brilliant general who led the Greeks to victory over many lands. His army and navy were greatly feared.

Greek statues are thrown out.

JUDAS MACCABAEUS

The Greeks wanted all defeated peoples to worship the Greek gods They even put statues in the Temple in Jerusalem. Judas Maccabaeus led a band of freedom fighters to restore the Temple for Jewish worship.

The scriptures are written on scrolls.

SCRIPTURE

In the time of the foreign empires, many Jews lived far from Jerusalem. To stay true to their traditions, they wanted to be able to study their scriptures together. They began meeting in synagogues to hear the ancient stories read aloud.

THE NEW TESTAMENT is the second part of the Christian Bible. It tells of Jesus and his followers.

The followers of Jesus came to believe that he was God's chosen one – the king who, like David, would set his people free. They would then be able to live as God's people should.

The word they used for king is 'Christ'.

New Testament

Jesus is born

Luke 1–2

The little town of Nazareth clings to a hilltop in the region of Galilee. Long ago, it was home to a young woman named Mary. She was looking forward to getting married. Her husband-to-be was named Joseph.

One day, God sent the angel Gabriel to give her a message.

'May you have peace and joy!' said the angel. 'God has blessed you.'

Mary was overcome with awe. Who was this messenger? What did the words mean?

'Don't be afraid,' said Gabriel. 'God has chosen you to be the mother of a special child: you will name him "Jesus".

'He will be a king like the great King David – the

one who, long ago, ruled your people and rescued them from their enemies.

'Jesus' kingdom will last for ever.'

Mary felt as if her breath had been taken away. When she did speak, it was barely a whisper.

'That can't be true,' she said. 'I'm a virgin – not yet married.'

'God will make it come true,' said the angel. 'Your child will be God's own Son.'

Mary bowed her head. 'I am ready to do what God wants,' she said.

At this time, the land of the Jewish people was actually ruled by foreigners. It was part of the vast Roman empire.

The emperor, Augustus, had just ordered a census. He wanted everyone to put their details on a special register. Then he would be able to work out who needed to pay taxes and how much.

Joseph and Mary agreed to register together: after all, they were soon to be married and they would then be family.

The emperor wanted everyone to register in their home town, so Mary and Joseph set off for Bethlehem. It was famous as the birthplace of King David, and Joseph was proud that he was descended from the nation's greatest leader.

After a journey of several days, they arrived. Bethlehem was full of visitors. There was no room anywhere – the local inn was fully booked. Mary and Joseph had no choice but to shelter in a stable.

While they were there, the time came for Mary to have her baby. She wrapped him in the traditional baby clothes called swaddling. Then she laid him in a manger as proudly as if it had been a proper cradle.

Out in the fields nearby, some shepherds were wide awake. They were keeping watch over their flocks of sheep all through the dark and dangerous night.

Suddenly, they gasped with fear. Something they had never seen before shone out in front of them like a bright, white fire.

There, in the glittering light, stood one of God's angels.

The shepherds huddled back into the shadows. They were desperate to find a hiding place.

'Don't be afraid,' cried the angel. 'I bring you good news – news to make the whole world laugh and sing. Tonight, in David's town, God's new king has been born.

'He is the one who will lead you to freedom: the one who will make the whole world new.

'Go and see him! He's wrapped in swaddling clothes and lying in a manger.'

All at once, hundreds and thousands of angels appeared and they burst out singing:

'*Glory to God in heaven;*
Peace on earth.'

The angels' melody rang across the skies, wilder and more wonderful than any music the shepherds had ever heard.

Then, as suddenly as they had appeared, the angels vanished into heaven.

The shepherds looked at one another. They were too shaken to speak.

Then one shouted, 'Come on! Let's go and find out if any of this is true.'

They hurried off to Bethlehem, peering in through doorways and windows wherever they saw a glimmer of light.

At last they found Mary and Joseph and saw the baby in the manger.

'Let us tell you about what we saw!' they said. 'Heaven's angels told us all about your newborn son and the wonderful things he will do.'

Mary listened hard. She wanted to remember everything the shepherds said. She wanted to treasure the words for ever.

Babies and children

In Bible times, people could not afford to let babies and young children get in the way of working for a living!

Children looked after the family's flock of sheep.

Sometimes bab are put in a hammock

Mostly, children joined in with the grown-ups' jobs.

Playing soldiers.

:ching baby
le playing
flute.

Helping
in the
home.

A mother carries her
swaddled baby in a
sling.

Playing weddings.

Young children amused
themselves with simple games.

Toys on wheels

Balls

King Herod and the newborn king

Matthew 2

At the time when Jesus was born, King Herod was in charge of the land of the Jews.

Herod liked to think of himself as a great king: he had built palaces and fortresses to show everyone that he was rich and powerful. He had arranged for the Temple in Jerusalem to be rebuilt so that religious Jews would support him.

Even so, he knew that his job was not safe. His own relatives were jealous of him, and he knew that some might plot against him. Besides, the emperor in Rome had the final say about everything: at any moment he could choose someone else to be king.

So he was not pleased when his private guards brought him this news:

'Your Majesty, some visitors are causing quite a stir here in Jerusalem. They are scholars from lands far to the east. They say they have seen a new star in the sky and that it has led them here.

'They say the star is a sign that a new king has been born… someone who will be the king of the Jews.'

King Herod called a meeting of all the important people who might know something useful.

'Listen,' he said to them. 'There's been talk about God sending a great king to the Jewish people for years – hundreds of years, in fact. I know that the ancient books of our people talk about this king. Now tell me, what exactly do they say? Where is this king going to be born?'

'In Bethlehem,' the priests replied eagerly. 'The book of the prophet Micah is quite clear.'

They read the treasured words aloud.

'That's all I need from you then,' Herod interrupted. 'You may go.'

Alone with his private guards, he barked another order: 'Fetch those visitors. I'll expect them here tonight.'

A few hours later, in a lamplit room in the palace, King Herod listened to all the visitors had to say about the star.

He leaned forward. 'I've been doing my best to

242

help you,' he said. 'I've found out that the king will
be born in Bethlehem.

'Now I'd like you to help me: go there, find the
king, and then come back here. I want to show my
respect for him too; however, it is important that my
visit be a surprise.'

The scholars from the east set out at once.

'Look!' said one. 'There's the star. It's leading us to Bethlehem. Everything is working out perfectly.'

And so it was. The star dipped low over one little house in Bethlehem. Inside they found Mary and her baby son.

At once, they knelt down and paid homage. It seemed to each of them that the little boy was already the greatest king in all the world.

Then they brought out rich gifts. 'Here is gold,'
said one, 'the symbol of royal power.'

'Here is frankincense,' said the second, 'the symbol
of someone who is a priest to his people and brings
them close to God.'

'Here is myrrh,' said the third, 'the symbol of
healing: in your son's kingdom, everyone will be
made well.'

Soon after, the scholars got ready to leave.

'You know,' said one, 'I've been having troubling dreams. I believe they are warning me about King Herod. I'm afraid he thinks that this child is a rival, and wants to harm him.'

'How odd! I've been waking in the night thinking exactly the same,' said the second.

'So have I,' said the third, 'but I decided not to say anything after Herod seemed so helpful.'

The scholars agreed that Herod's helpfulness was a

sham, and they set off for their own country along a road that did not pass by Jerusalem.

That night, Joseph had a dream so terrifying it shook him awake.

'Come!' he whispered to Mary. 'We must keep Jesus safe from Herod. God is telling me that we should go to Egypt. We must go now.'

They hurried to gather their few possessions and set off just as dawn was breaking.

As Joseph turned for one last look at Bethlehem, he saw a troop of Herod's soldiers marching through the gate, swords at the ready.

He had been only just in time to save his much-loved family. It was going to be some time before he dared go back to Nazareth.

Trades and crafts

In Bible times, sons learned the family trade. Jesus would have learned carpentry skills from Joseph. A carpenter was a master builder, as well as someone who worked with wood.

CARPENTER

The carpenter makes and mends all kinds of wooden items.

Furnace

Bringing cloth to market.

A carpenter mends the roof.

BLACKSMITH

POTTER

Clay

Bellows

Wheel

A potter sells his wares
from his workshop.

The blacksmith makes
metal tools.

Kiln

249

The boy Jesus

Luke 2

The most important festival of the Jewish year was Passover. It was the time when people listened once again to the stories of Moses. They thought about God's laws and what it meant to be God's people.

The very best place to celebrate Passover was at the Temple in Jerusalem. Every year, Jesus' parents used to go there from Nazareth, along with many other pilgrims.

When Jesus was twelve years old, he was allowed to go too. He saw the ceremonies in the Temple. He sat around the table with his family and friends from Nazareth to enjoy the Passover meal.

All too soon, it was time to go home. Everyone laughed and chattered as they walked along the dusty road, and the hours flew by.

When they stopped for the night, Mary began looking for Jesus.

'Where can he have got to?' she said, and she sounded exasperated.

'Boys!' she complained to a friend. 'I'm sure I saw them all larking around most of the day. But at least the others came back to their families as soon as there was food on offer!'

The trouble was, Jesus hadn't been larking around with the other boys. He hadn't been with the party of pilgrims at all that day. And his mother simply hadn't noticed.

He wasn't with the group.

'We'll have to go back to Jerusalem,' she explained tearfully to her friends.

She and her husband hurried back to the city as fast as they could, and began searching. They went to the place where they had stayed; to the market streets with their laden stalls; through the tiny, twisting streets where it was so easy to get lost.

Then they went to the Temple. Its vast courtyard was crowded with pilgrims and sightseers alike. Slowly they edged their way through.

There, in a shady colonnade, they found their son. Jesus was with a group of scholars. They were talking about the stories of Moses and about God's laws and what it meant to be God's people.

'What are you doing here?' cried Mary, as she rushed to hug him. 'We've been frantic looking for you.'

Jesus replied with genuine surprise. 'Why did you have to look for me? Didn't you know I would be in my Father's house?'

Mary shook her head with disbelief. 'You tell him,' she said to her husband. 'I'm too upset to argue. Tell him his home is with us in Nazareth.'

Jesus smiled. 'Anyway, I'm coming with you now,' he said.

And so he went, and grew up a good and obedient son.

Jesus' new beginning

Luke 3–4

All of a sudden, making a new beginning seemed to be quite the fashion. And that was all because of a rather unusual preacher named John.

John's parents had lived perfectly ordinary lives. His father, Zechariah, was a priest, and his mother, Elizabeth (who was Mary's cousin), had been

devoted to her only child.

But John was different. He dressed in rough clothes, like a prophet from days of old. He chose to live out in the wild country. The message he preached was fierce and direct.

Crowds came to listen to him, curious to find out for themselves what he was like.

'Get ready for God!' he cried. 'Live as God's people should!'

'What does that mean?' the crowd wanted to know.

'Stop grasping for money,' he replied. 'Share what you have with the poor. Be fair to everyone in everything you do.'

Many people were deeply moved by his words.

'We do want to live as God's people,' they decided. 'Please perform the ceremony of a new beginning, and baptize us in water.'

John agreed, and he became famous for baptizing many people in the River Jordan.

It didn't take long before the gossip about John became very excitable.

'Do you think he's the special king God has promised?' his followers began to whisper. 'Do you think he's the one that people will call Messiah and Christ?'

John found out what they were saying.

'I'm not the messiah,' he told them firmly. 'When he comes, you will all see that he is much greater than I am. He will have God's power to change everything.'

Not long after, Jesus himself came to John and asked to be baptized.

John recognized Jesus and was puzzled. 'You don't need to make a new beginning,' he said. 'If anything, I should be asking you to give me a new beginning.'

But Jesus asked John again, and John agreed.

He dipped Jesus beneath the water of the River Jordan and then lifted him up into the clear air.

What John saw next was something he would

remember always: something like a sunbeam shone down brightly, as if a curtain between heaven and earth had been pulled aside.

He heard a voice from heaven: 'This is my own dear Son, and I am pleased with him.'

Then a pure white dove fluttered down and sat on Jesus' head.

After he was baptized, Jesus went off by himself further into the wild country.

For forty days he went without food and spent all his time thinking and praying.

Then the devil, who brings wicked thoughts, came and spoke to him.

'Just think how hungry you are! If you were God's Son, you could order these stones to turn to bread.'

Jesus answered at once: 'I've studied the special books of our people. They say quite clearly that people don't need just bread; they need the wisdom of God's word.'

Soon after, the devil spoke again. 'Picture yourself in Jerusalem,' said the devil, 'standing on the highest part of the Temple. If you were God's Son, you could throw yourself off. The angels would fly in to save you. Everyone would believe in you then.'

'I won't,' replied Jesus. 'This is what the special books of our people say: "Don't put God to the test."'

A third time the devil came to whisper to Jesus. 'Imagine all the kingdoms of the world. How splendid they are! If you bow down and say that I am your master, I'll put you in charge of all of them.'

'I won't,' replied Jesus. 'God's laws are clear. We must worship God alone.'

A chill breeze riffled through the dust. As it passed, the devil simply vanished.

The land of Jesus

All that Jesus said and did happened in a very small part of the world.
From Bethlehem to Mount Hermon is only some 100 kilometres.

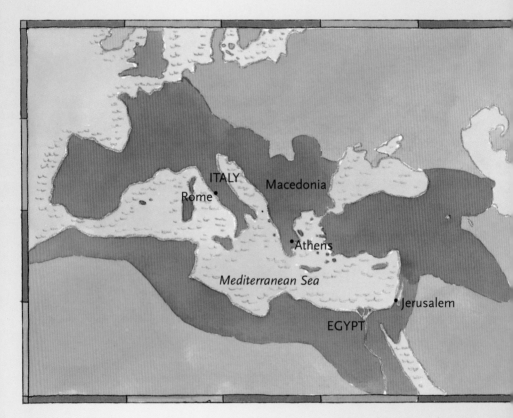

The red area shows the extent of the
Roman empire around the time of Jesus.

MOUNT HERMON

Mediterranean Sea

Most of Jesus'
teaching took
place in the
region of Galilee.

GALILEE

Capernaum

Magdala

Lake Galilee

Nazareth

SAMARIA

River Jordan

— Travellers from
the east would
have come by this
route.

Jesus was
crucified
just outside
the city walls
of Jerusalem.

— This line traces
the likely route
from Nazareth to
Bethlehem.

JUDAEA

Emmaus

Jericho

Jerusalem

Bethany

Bethlehem

Dead Sea

261

Jesus and his followers

Matthew 4, 9–10

Jesus had made up his mind. He was going to begin the work that God was calling him to do.

He was going to tell people how to live as God's friends; he was going to show people how to live as God's friends.

He left his home in Nazareth and made a new home for himself in Capernaum, down on the shore

of Lake Galilee. Every day, he went out and about preaching and teaching.

'My message is good news,' he told his listeners. 'Stop doing the things that spoil your friendship with God. It is time to live as God's people should, as part of God's new kingdom.'

Jesus did more than just talk about God's new kingdom. He was also able to work miracles.

With just a touch, he healed those who were sick. With just a word, he calmed those who had been held in the grip of madness.

His many wonderful deeds helped people to believe that God's power was truly at work.

One day, as he was walking along the shore of Lake Galilee, he saw two fishermen casting their nets. They were brothers: Simon and Andrew.

'Come with me,' said Jesus. 'I want you to help me with the work I am doing. You won't be catching fish any more. You will be gathering people into God's kingdom.'

At once, the two brothers left their nets and followed him.

A little further on, he saw two other brothers; James and John were getting into their fishing boat with their father Zebedee. 'Come with me!' Jesus called. 'Join us in the work we are going to do to help people live as God's friends.'

The two men left their nets, their boat and their father to be with Jesus.

Jesus continued to spread his message and work miracles. Soon, he needed more helpers.

One day, when he was preaching to a large crowd, he noticed a wealthy man sitting in his booth in the marketplace.

It was the local tax collector. Nobody liked tax collectors very much. That was partly because they worked for the Romans who ruled the land; it was also partly because they charged everyone more money than was right or fair.

But Jesus could see what the man was like. 'Matthew,' he said, 'I want you to come and follow me.'

The tax collector was delighted. He held a feast to celebrate. He introduced Jesus to all his tax collector friends.

They were delighted to meet him.

'Imagine,' they whispered among themselves. 'Here's a preacher who doesn't mind spending time with us.'

'Religious types usually stay as far away from us as possible.'

'Yet this Jesus is even saying we can be friends with God! The God he talks about must be very forgiving, when you think of some of the things we get up to.'

In fact, many more people were eager to listen to Jesus and to count themselves as his followers.

Soon, Jesus chose twelve of his followers to be his closest friends and helpers: his disciples.

There were the four fishermen: Simon, who was usually known as Peter, and three more – Andrew, James and John.

Then there was Matthew the tax collector.

After that Jesus had chosen Philip, Bartholomew, Thomas, another James and Thaddaeus.

He had also chosen a freedom fighter named Simon, and a twelfth person who was especially good at looking after the money the group needed. His name was Judas Iscariot.

A group of women also became Jesus' close supporters.

Mary Magdalene was devoted to Jesus because he had made her well.

Joanna thought Jesus' teaching was wiser and more important than any of the government talk that her husband brought back from his job at the royal court.

Susanna was a wealthy woman who was able to choose exactly how she spent her money. She decided to give large amounts to helping Jesus, so he and his friends could spend all their time preaching and teaching.

The crowd of people who followed Jesus grew and grew: there were young and old, men and women, rich and poor. Jesus welcomed them and invited them all to be part of God's kingdom.

Everyday life in Capernaum

When Jesus became a teacher and preacher, his home base was the town of Capernaum beside Lake Galilee.

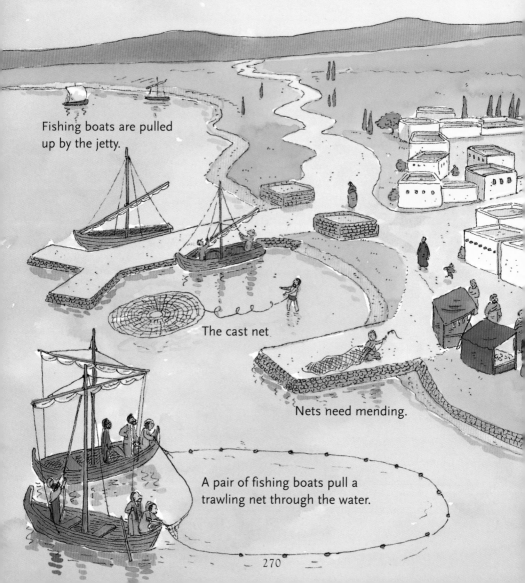

Fishing boats are pulled up by the jetty.

The cast net

Nets need mending.

A pair of fishing boats pull a trawling net through the water.

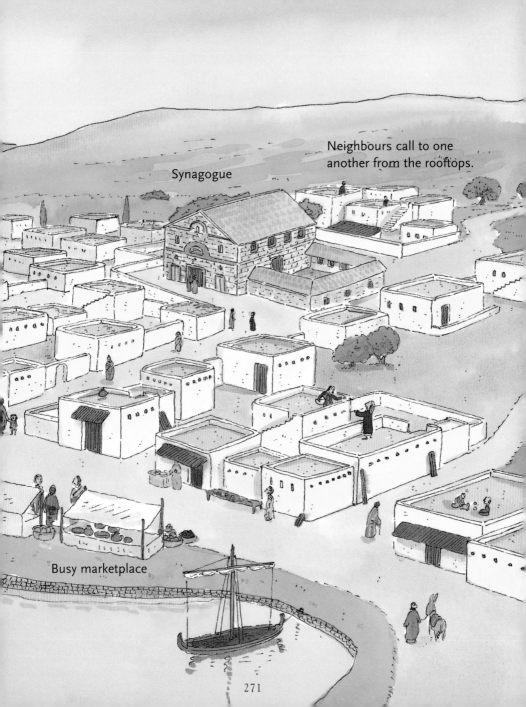

Synagogue

Neighbours call to one another from the rooftops.

Busy marketplace

Jesus and the Pharisees

Mark 2–3; Luke 5–6

Among the Jewish people were those who called themselves Pharisees. They tried to be as faithful as they could possibly be to God's laws.

They were curious to find out about Jesus; after all, he was very popular with the crowds.

But they were also a bit worried. They were not entirely sure that Jesus was explaining God's laws properly.

One day, they arranged to come and meet Jesus. They chose to meet in someone's house, and the room was soon crowded.

Even so, more and more people kept arriving. They crowded into the courtyard and jostled by the gate.

Then yet more people arrived: a group of men who were carrying a friend on his sleeping mat.

'If we can get you to Jesus, perhaps he'll be able to make you well,' they explained. 'He's already cured people who were paralysed like you.'

'But we can't even get near the door,' groaned the paralysed man.

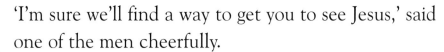

'I'm sure we'll find a way to get you to see Jesus,' said one of the men cheerfully.

'I know how these houses are put together. Come on: up the steps to the flat roof. We'll make a new door to the room.'

The owners of the house had a garden and sitting area on the roof. There, under the shade of the fig tree, the friends began to take the roof apart.

Then the man who had had the idea in the first place found some rope.

He began knotting it to the four corners of his friend's sleeping mat.

'This is how the plan is going to work,' he explained. 'We've scraped the roof away as far as the ceiling. We're going to pick up our friend on his bed,' and here the man raised his head in alarm, 'and let it down quite fast. That'll break the ceiling plaster.

'Then you,' and here he turned to the man on his bed, 'must keep lying still while we lower you into the room where Jesus is.'

'How do you get me out again?' asked the paralysed man.

'I'm quite sure you'll walk out,' came the reply.

The Pharisees and the teachers of the Law stood up in alarm as the ceiling crashed down.

Jesus seemed to find the whole thing rather more amusing. After all, he'd spent his growing-up years as a carpenter and had worked on building sites.

He smiled as he saw the man being lowered to the floor in front of him. He grinned at the hopeful faces of the men on the roof. He knew they had total faith in him.

'Well,' he said to the man, 'your sins are forgiven.'

At once the murmuring began. 'Only God can forgive sins,' the Pharisees whispered. 'Just saying those words is a wicked thing to do.'

Jesus turned to them. 'It's easy to say, "Your sins are forgiven,"' he said. 'It's harder to say, "Get up and walk" because everyone can tell whether or not the words meant anything.

'Now I'm going to prove that I do have God's authority to say that someone's sins are forgiven.'

He turned to the man on his bed. 'Get up,' he said. 'Pick up your bed and go home.'

To everyone's amazement, the paralysed man got up and almost danced away, singing and laughing.

The Pharisees and the teachers of the Law were astonished.

'It is very wrong of Jesus to say he can forgive sins,' they agreed. 'That's like saying you're equal with God. That's against the Law.'

Soon, they were hearing other stories that made them even angrier.

'You know the Law about resting on the sabbath day? Jesus doesn't keep that one either. People saw him walking through a cornfield one sabbath, and he let his disciples pick ears of corn and eat the grains. That's working. It's harvesting – not the whole field, of course, only a few handfuls, but it's still harvesting. And it's not allowed on the sabbath.'

'There's worse,' said another. 'Another sabbath, Jesus went to a synagogue for the sabbath day service. He was invited to preach there. He saw a man with a paralysed hand, and he called him to the front. Then he asked a direct question: "What does the Law allow us to do on the Sabbath: to help or to harm?"'

'Well, we said nothing. We could see where that one was going. Then, in front of everyone, he told the man to lift his bad arm. Jesus had healed it. That's more work. More lawbreaking.'

They began to talk about what they could do to stop Jesus.

The Jewish faith in the time of Jesus

In the time of Jesus, the Jewish people met for worship on the sabbath day in a building called a synagogue. There were teachers, called rabbis, who helped explain the scriptures – the Law of Moses and the words of the prophets. Many rabbis belonged to a very strict religious group called the Pharisees.

THE SYNAGOGUE SCHOOL
Here boys were taught to read the scriptures.

The rabbi wears a prayer shawl.

Writing is done on wooden tablets filled with wax that can be used again.

INSIDE THE SYNAGOGUE

The Jews gathered for worship in the synagogue on the weekly day of rest, the sabbath.

Cupboard containing the scriptures

Seven-branched lampstand like the one made for the tabernacle

The rabbi reads from a scroll.

Men sit on one side, women and children on the other.

Wise words of Jesus

Matthew 5–7

One day, Jesus saw huge crowds of people coming to listen to him. He walked out into the countryside until he found a place where there was room for everyone to sit down. Then he began to preach.

'Is there anyone here who wants to live as God's friend – who wants to do that more than anything else? Here is good news: God will make your dream come true.

'No one is to think that I've come to get rid of the old laws that God gave our people. If you want to be friends with God, you will need to be more faithful to the Law than the Pharisees.

'The Law tells us we should be fair in punishing people: an eye for an eye, a tooth for a tooth. I am telling you a better way: don't seek revenge. If someone hits you on one cheek, let them hit the other. If someone asks you to carry their stuff for one mile, offer to carry it for two.

'The Law says you should love your friends and hate your enemies. I am telling you a better way: love your enemies as well. Even the people who don't believe in God are nice to their friends. You must be ready to be good and kind towards everyone.

'Always remember to pray to God, but do so quietly and without showing off. Say these words:

Our Father in heaven:
May everyone show respect for you and your holy name.
May everyone do the things that are pleasing to you.
Give us the food and strength we need to face each day.
Forgive us when we do wrong.
Remind us to forgive others.
Keep us safe from discouragement and danger.

'Don't spend your life worrying about money and the things it can buy.

'Look at the birds: they don't sow seeds or gather a harvest. Even so, God takes care of them.

'Look at the wild flowers: they don't worry about what to wear. And yet their petals are lovely – more wonderful and intricate than really expensive clothes.

'So stop fretting about food and clothes and things like that. Make it your aim to do what God wants and to live as a friend of God – part of God's kingdom.

'I want you to listen to what I say and obey my teaching.

'If you do, you will be like a wise builder.

'The wise builder chooses the right place for his house. The rain may come. The wind may howl. The rivers may flood. But his house stands firm because it is built on solid rock.

'If you listen to what I say and simply forget about it, you will be like a foolish builder.

'The foolish builder simply chooses the easy place to put up a house. When the rain pours down and the gales roar and the rivers spill over their banks, his house falls flat.'

Jesus' listeners were impressed. 'He sounds as if he really knows what he's talking about,' they said. 'The other teachers of the Law never sound convincing in the way that Jesus does.'

The Romans

In the time of Jesus, the Romans ruled their empire from Rome. Their soldiers were everywhere. In fact, many Jews hoped that God would send a king like David – a messiah – who would fight to set them free.

PONTIUS PILATE
This Roman was governor in Jerusalem in the time of Jesus.

Coins bear the likeness of the Roman emperor.

This Jewish tax collector is handing over money to the governor.

Rebels and freedom fighters are whipped and put to death by crucifixion.

ANTONIA FORTRESS
The garrison in Jerusalem
was next to the Temple.

Roman
soldiers force
locals to carry
their packs.

A God-fearing Roman
soldier exchanges a
greeting with a local
rabbi.

The soldier's
slave wears an
identity badge.

The parable of the sower

Matthew 13; Mark 4

One day, Jesus began to speak down by the shore of
Lake Galilee. So many people came to
listen to him that there was
nowhere left for him to stand
and be seen. So he climbed into
a boat that was a little way out
in the water and spoke to the
crowds from there.

He began to tell a story.
'Listen,' he said. 'There was
once a man who went out to sow
his crops. He walked up and down
the furrowed field, scattering handfuls of seeds as
he went.

'Some fell on the path where the earth was packed hard. The wild birds swooped down for a feast.

'Some seeds fell on rocky ground where the soil was shallow. They soon sprouted, but their roots could not reach down into moist earth. When the days grew hot, the new green leaves shrivelled away.

'Some seeds fell among thorn bushes. The young plants began to grow, but the thorns choked them of light and moisture, and they produced nothing.

'Some seeds fell in good soil. They sprouted and grew and produced full ears of grain – some thirty, some sixty, some a hundred.

'Listen!' Jesus reminded them. 'Listen out for the meaning in my story.'

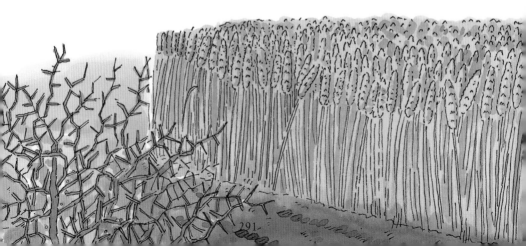

In a quiet moment, Jesus' twelve disciples came to speak to him. They looked a bit sheepish.

'We don't understand the story,' they confessed. 'Can you explain it, please?'

Jesus gave a sigh, like a teacher whose pupils need yet another explanation of something rather simple.

'Think of it like this,' he said. 'The sower is sowing God's message. Some of it falls on the path. The people there hear the message, but then Satan comes and snatches it away.

'Some of it falls on rocky ground. The people there are excited by the message and begin to change their lives to be part of God's kingdom. Then things get tough. They get bullied and mocked – and they give up.

'Some of it falls among thorn bushes. The people there hear God's message and are convinced by it.

The problem is that all the things of
everyday life get in the way. They
end up worrying more about
money than about following God.
'Some of the message falls on
good soil. The people there hear
God's message and are changed
by it. Their lives produce a harvest
of good deeds – some thirty, some
sixty, some a hundred.'
Jesus nodded to his disciples and then went back to
preaching to the crowds. He had
many stories to tell, and he
trusted that at least some
of his listeners would
understand their
meaning.

The farming year

Throughout Bible times, people relied on a good harvest each year. Even city-dwellers were very aware of the farming year.

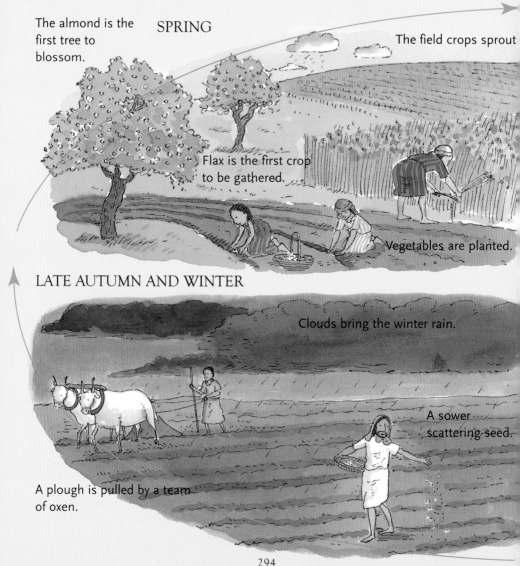

The almond is the first tree to blossom.

SPRING

The field crops sprout

Flax is the first crop to be gathered.

Vegetables are planted.

LATE AUTUMN AND WINTER

Clouds bring the winter rain.

A sower scattering seed.

A plough is pulled by a team of oxen.

SUMMER

The threshing sledge chops the ears of grain from the stalks.

Wheat

Barley

Vines are tended.

Winnowing separates the chaff and the grain.

Apricots

HARVEST

Almonds

Olives are beaten from the tree.

The storm on the lake

Mark 4

Jesus had had a long and weary day preaching to the crowds.

'Let's go away for some time by ourselves,' he said to his disciples. 'Let's take the boat across the lake to the far shore.'

Those of his friends who had been fishermen took charge of the sail and the steering oar. Even though people tried to keep up with them in boats, they went faster and further out towards the middle of the lake.

Jesus found a space at the back of the boat and lay down with his head on a pillow. Soon he was fast asleep.

Then, as the last of the light faded, a strong wind began to blow. It rocked the sturdy little boat, and rattled the mast. Then a giant wave crashed over the bow.

'Get the sail down fast!' ordered Peter. 'Those who know how, get the oars out and row. Everyone else, grab a bucket and start bailing. We're heading for the nearest land.'

Everyone began working frantically, but the storm only got worse.

'Do you think we're going to make it?' shouted someone, their voice shrill with panic.

'Wake Jesus!' shrieked another. 'Why isn't he helping? Doesn't he care?'

The man almost threw himself at Jesus and shook him awake.

Jesus sat up sleepily. Almost at once he had to grab
the edge of the boat to steady himself. All around
him his friends were yelling and the wind was
roaring.

He rubbed his eyes and stood up.

'Hush,' he said to the waves. 'Be still,' he said to
the wind.

The little boat shuddered to a stop. The wind flew
away and the waves shivered into ripples.
A silver moon slid out from behind
a dark and ragged cloud.

Jesus turned to his friends. 'Why were you afraid?' he asked. 'Don't you have faith in me?'

He shrugged and lay down to sleep again. Peter motioned to his fisherman friends to help him raise the sail. A gentle breeze began to carry the boat on its way.

Slowly, the men doing the bailing scooped out the last of the water. Then they mopped the floor of the boat dry.

One by one, they found a place to sit. They looked at one another uneasily. Then they all began looking at Jesus. Fear and suspicion was written all over their faces.

'So,' said someone, 'who is this Jesus we've agreed to support?

'Who can he really be? Even the wind and the waves obey him!'

Jairus and his daughter

Mark 5; Luke 8

Jairus stood anxiously on the quayside. Like everyone else, he was watching the little boat sailing into the harbour. Jesus was returning to their town, and people were eager to see him.

As soon as Jesus was on dry land, Jairus rushed to get close to him. He threw himself at Jesus' feet, almost sobbing.

'Please come quickly,' he begged. 'My only daughter is dying. She's only twelve. Please help me.'

'Of course I'll come,' said Jesus.

Jairus tried to lead the way through the jostling crowds, but it was slow going. When he glanced back, he saw that Jesus wasn't pushing at all.

Then Jesus stopped completely.

'Someone touched me,' he said. 'Who was it?'

Jesus' voice was stern. No one replied.

'Who knows!' said Peter. 'Everyone was grabbing at you.'

'No, someone touched me on purpose,' said Jesus. 'It felt different.'

A woman stepped forward. 'I'm sorry,' she said. 'It was me. I've been unwell for years, and I just hoped… but I only touched your cloak. That wasn't the wrong thing to do, was it?'

Jesus smiled. 'Of course not,' he said. 'You have shown great faith, and for that reason you are healed.'

At that moment, someone came hurrying with a message for Jairus.

'I'm sorry,' he announced solemnly. 'There's no need to bother the Teacher any more.'

Jairus stared at him bleakly and began to tremble. The messenger nodded slowly.

'Your daughter died just a little while ago,' he said. 'We have begun to arrange the funeral.'

Jairus buried his face in his hands and began sobbing. Then he heard Jesus speaking to him: 'Don't be afraid. Only believe, and she will be well. Come on, lead the way to your house.'

As they got nearer, they could hear the sound of wailing. Women had arrived at Jairus's house to sing the traditional songs of grief.

'Don't cry,' said Jesus. 'The girl is only sleeping.'

One of the women shrieked angrily at him. 'Don't talk nonsense! Show some kindness and respect at a time like this. The girl is dead, for sure.'

'Take me to the girl's room,' said Jesus to Jairus. 'Your wife must come too, of course; and please allow three of my companions to be there as well.'

They walked out of the sunlight and into the dark room where the little girl still lay on her bed.

Jesus walked over to the frail body. Gently he lifted the little girl's pale hand.

'Come on, get up,' he said softly.

Behind him, the girl's mother gasped. 'Jairus, she's moving,' she said.

The girl sighed and stretched as if waking from a deep dream. She then wriggled and sat up, clasping her knees.

'Oh!' she said, in astonishment. 'What's everyone doing here?'

She looked at her mother. 'What's the time? Have I been asleep long? Is it time to eat yet?'

Her mother was laughing and crying all at once as she hugged her daughter. Jairus went round hugging everyone else, stopping every now and then to wipe his eyes on his sleeve.

'I think you'd better get a meal ready at once!' said

Jesus. 'Your daughter must be hungry.'

'Oh, we must have a party and tell everyone what's happened!' Jairus exclaimed. 'You must be there as well so we can thank you in public.'

Jesus shook his head. 'I don't want you to talk about what I've done,' he said. 'As for me and my friends, we must get on with our work.'

And with that, they were on their way, leaving behind them a household brimming with joy and laughter.

Who is Jesus?

Luke 9

Every day, Jesus spent time praying to God. He always went to a quiet place where he could be alone.

One day, when he had finished praying, he had a question for his disciples.

'The crowds who follow me,' he said, 'who do they say I am?'

'They think you're a prophet,' came the instant

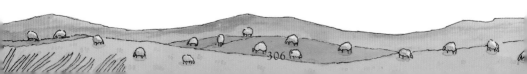

reply. 'Some say you must be one of the great prophets of old come back to life. It's clear you have wisdom from God.'

Jesus looked at his friends thoughtfully. 'Who do you say I am?' he asked.

Peter had his answer ready. 'You are God's chosen king,' he said. 'You should be called Messiah or Christ.'

It was an announcement of huge importance. Jesus gathered the group of friends closer round him.

'You mustn't talk about this to anyone,' he said. 'You already know that my teaching has made enemies. The religious leaders – the Pharisees, the teachers of the Law, the Temple priests – they all mistrust me. In the end, they'll have me executed, I'm sure.

'Now, I know in my heart that God will not allow me to rot in the grave. But you need to know that following me is going to be dangerous. There's a price to being part of God's kingdom.'

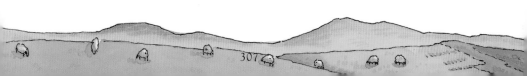

About a week later, Jesus went with Peter, John and James to the top of a high mountain.

Jesus found a quiet place to say his prayers. His friends lay down in the sunshine and fell asleep.

Suddenly, they were startled awake: a dazzling light seemed to be shining from heaven itself. Jesus' clothes became shining white, and even his face looked different.

Two men were talking to Jesus. The disciples recognized them as two of the greatest prophets from days gone by: Moses and Elijah.

They were talking about the things that needed to happen for all that God planned to come true.

Peter was thrilled by the sight.

'Master,' he cried, 'we should make this mountain top a place of worship for you all!'

While he was speaking, a cloud came and settled over everything. Suddenly, everything was hidden.

The disciples heard a voice: 'This is my Son, whom I have chosen. Listen to him.'

Then everything fell quiet. The cloud lifted and there was Jesus, all alone, as if nothing had happened.

The disciples glanced at one another. They knew what they had seen, but they also knew it would be better to say nothing about it.

The Good Samaritan

Luke 10

One day, a teacher of the Law came to see Jesus. 'I'd like to find out more about your teaching,' he said eagerly. 'There's one question that I think is key to our faith. What must I do to have eternal life?'

Jesus looked him in the eye. He was sure the man was little more than a spy, sent to trick him into saying something against the Law. He replied with a question.

'What do our special writings tell us? What do you think they mean?'

'Oh, the writings are clear,' said the man. 'Love God with every part of your being, and love the person next to you as much as you love yourself.'

'Quite right,' said Jesus. 'Do that, and you will have eternal life.'

The teacher of the Law looked crestfallen but also slightly cross. His plan had failed. 'But… that's not as easy as it seems. Who is "the person next to me"?'

'I'll tell you a story,' said Jesus. 'There was once a man who was going from Jerusalem to Jericho. When he was on the lonely part of the road, some bandits sprang out and attacked him. They took all his belongings and left him for dead.

311

'It so happened that a priest from the Temple in Jerusalem came along. He saw the body on the road and hurried past, keeping as far away as he could.

'Then one of the Temple staff came along. He saw the body and stopped in his tracks. Cautiously, he stepped closer. Then, in a sudden panic, he raced away.

'Later, a businessman came along. He was from the region of Samaria – you know the place, with its religious traditions that are so unlike ours. When he saw the man, he knew he had to do something. He went over and treated the man's injuries. He lifted him onto his donkey and led him to an inn. There,

he settled him in comfortably and paid the innkeeper to look after him until such time as he was able to come back.'

The teacher of the Law looked uncomfortable. Jesus' story had deliberately included religious insiders and a religious outsider.

'So,' said Jesus, 'which of the three passers-by recognized that he was the person next to the poor victim on the road?'

'The one who helped him,' said the teacher, somewhat grumpily.

'Then follow that example,' said Jesus.

The two sisters

Luke 10

One day, Jesus and his disciples came to a small village.

A woman named Martha came hurrying to greet them. 'You must all come and stay at our house,' she said. 'It will be a pleasure to look after you.'

Jesus agreed readily, and Martha beamed with delight as she ushered her guests into a room and made sure they were comfortable.

'Now I'll go and prepare a meal,' she exclaimed.

First she had to fetch water.

Then she had to grind grain into flour to make bread.

Then she had to go and pick vegetables.

Suddenly she caught sight of her sister, Mary. She was sitting at Jesus' feet, listening as he preached.

Martha stood in the doorway, her hands on her hips.

'Excuse me, Jesus,' she said crossly. 'That sister of mine ought to be out here helping with the work. Tell her to come at once.'

Mary looked from Jesus to her sister and back again.

Jesus shook his head. 'Dear Martha,' he said. 'You're worried about so many things, but only one thing is important. Mary has chosen to listen to my teaching, and that is the very best thing to do.'

Lost and found

Luke 15

The crowds who came flocking to Jesus included all sorts of people.

Among the people he welcomed were tax collectors, who were hated for their greed and dishonesty.

The Pharisees and the teachers of the Law were most unhappy. 'How dare Jesus call himself a preacher,' they grumbled. 'It's against all our traditions to sit down to a meal with outcasts like them – yet he seems to enjoy their company.'

Jesus told them a story.

'Imagine you are a shepherd,' he said, 'and that you have a hundred sheep.

'One day, when you are counting them, you find there are only ninety-nine. What do you do?'

'You go and find the lost sheep,' called someone.

'You go and find it,' agreed Jesus. 'There's always

someone who can take care of the sheep in the pasture. As a good shepherd, you go and find the lost sheep.

'When at last you find it, it feels like a dream come true. You're so pleased, you have a big party.

'It's the same for people. When someone whose life has gone bad turns back to God, all heaven sings for joy.

'Now here's another story,' continued Jesus. 'There was once a man who had two sons.

'The younger son was eager to grow up and leave his family behind. He just needed money in order to pay his way.

'He went to his father. "Listen, Dad," he said. "You know you're wealthy, and you know that when you die, a share of what you have will come to me. I want to enjoy that money now. Go on, be reasonable!"

'The son nagged so much that his father finally agreed. The young man took the money and went off on his travels. He found a place to live in a faraway city and spent freely on all kinds of luxuries.

'Then things began to go wrong. There was a bad

harvest. The cost of living soared. The young man
ran out of money.

'He knew he'd have to get a job. There wasn't
much choice: everyone was facing hard times and
they couldn't afford extra workers.

'In the end, the young man found a farmer who was willing to hire him. He accepted a job looking after a herd of pigs.

'He felt dirty just looking at them, but he was so hungry, he felt tempted to eat some of their bean pods.

'He picked one up and turned it over in his hands. It even smelt of pigs.

'"This is ridiculous," he said to himself. "My father's servants are better off than I am.

'"I'm going to go back home and apologize to Dad. I'm going to admit that I've let him down and I've let God down too. Then I can ask him to hire me."

'He set off on the return journey, plodding the weary miles.

'He still had some way to go when he heard the sound of running. He looked up and saw his father, huffing and puffing with the effort of racing to hug him.

'"My dear, dear boy!" he exclaimed. "You're back! Oh, it's good to see you!"

'The son began his apology. "I've made a mess of everything," he mumbled. "I've let you down and I've let God down too. I don't deserve to be treated as a son, but I'd be grateful for a job on the farm."

'His father was hardly listening. "Hurry!" he called to his servants. "This boy needs something to wear to a party. We're going to have a feast."

'Meanwhile, the elder son was working in the fields. He had been loyal to his father all along.

'He came trudging home and heard the sound of music and dancing.

'He called to a servant who was busy roasting a whole animal over an open fire.

'"What's all this for?" he grumbled.

'"It's for your brother," said the servant. "Your father ordered us to take the best calf and cook it. He's got quite a party going."

'The elder brother scowled. "Did I hear you right?" he asked. "A party, for the arrogant young brat who went off wasting all his money on having a good time. That's outrageous! I'm not going near him."

'When the father found out that his elder son was so angry, he went to talk to him.

'"I've worked hard all these years and you've never let me have a party. What has my brother done to deserve all this?"

'The father hugged his elder son. "You are always

here with me, and everything I have is yours. But
your brother has come home. We thought he was lost
for ever, and we've found him." '

Flocks and cattle

When the Bible people were nomads, they had flocks with them all the time. When they lived as farmers, looking after the flocks and animals became a job on its own.

A shepherd leads his flock across the hills looking for pasture.

The sheepfold provides shelter at night. The shepherd sits in the gateway.

Only non-Jews would have kept pigs.

Cattle are highly prized and are kept in the field or barn.

The donkey is fed when it is not working.

Goats can thrive even in rough and rocky places.

Finding water is vital.

Jesus and the children

Mark 10; Luke 18

One day, Jesus' disciples were sitting in a group
together. When they saw them, the passers-by
nudged each other and whispered that this meant
that Jesus himself couldn't be far away.

The disciples gazed back at them, trying to look
aloof. Inside, they were feeling rather pleased at the
respect they were getting.

Then they heard a noise: a mixture of chattering,
laughing and shrieking all mixed up with the sound
of mothers scolding and cajoling.

It was a group of mothers and children, and they
were coming nearer. The disciples stood up.

'We've come to see Jesus,' said one of the mothers.
'We'd like him to say a little blessing prayer for our
children.'

The disciples were scornful in their reply. 'You do
understand that Jesus is very, very busy, don't you?

All kinds of people need to talk to him about important matters, you know. He hasn't got time for fun and games.'

The mothers looked crestfallen. The children fell silent. A baby began to wail.

Then Jesus came along and saw what was happening.

'Let the children come!' he said to his disciples. 'The kingdom of God belongs to children like this. In fact, anyone who wants to be part of God's kingdom must enter it in the same way a child does.'

A very short man

Luke 19

Everyone in Jericho was in a state of high excitement.

'Jesus is coming! Jesus is coming!'

'Look! You can see his party walking down the hill. It won't be long before he's in the city.'

'Come on – there are loads of people out by the roadside already. You want to see him, don't you?'

Everyone wanted to see Jesus. Even the local tax collector, Zacchaeus.

The trouble was, Zacchaeus was very short. More than that, his habit of overcharging had made him as unpopular as it had made him wealthy. So everyone was quite keen to make sure he was kept at the back of the crowd – where, as it happened, he could see nothing.

'I know how to beat that crowd,' Zacchaeus said to himself as he hurried further along the road. 'I was always good at tree climbing as a boy and… yes, this sycamore is easy to climb and will give me a great view.'

He swung himself up into the tree and sat on a branch among the leaves. He watched with interest as the famous preacher came near, and wondered what everyone thought was so special about him.

Then Jesus stopped – right under the tree.

'Hello there,' he called. 'Zacchaeus, I'd like to stay with you while I'm in Jericho.'

Zacchaeus nearly fell out of the tree. He clambered down as quickly as he could, trying not to hear the murmuring around him. The people in the crowd were not pleased.

'Can you believe it!' they were grumbling. 'Jesus is going to stay with that dirty cheat of a tax collector.'

'That's not my idea of what a great religious leader does. My opinion of Jesus has changed for the worse, I can tell you!'

Jesus paid no attention. He went cheerfully to Zacchaeus's elegant home and sat down to enjoy a fine meal.

Something in what he said changed the little tax collector for ever.

Zacchaeus stood up after the meal to give a speech. 'Listen, everyone,' he said to his guests. 'I am making this promise to Jesus and to you all. I'm going to give half my belongings to the poor. I'm going to pay back the people I have cheated – I shall give them back four times what I took.'

Jesus smiled approvingly. 'Today,' he said, 'this man
has been saved. He is one of God's people, and now
he is going to live as God's friend. That is what my
work is all about.'

A feast

Throughout Bible times, most food and drink was produced locally.
Only the wealthy could afford specialities from far away.

For the Jews, there were also strict food laws dating back to the time
of Moses. Some foods, such as pork, were considered 'unclean', and it
was forbidden for Jews to eat with non-Jews.

A PARTY AT THE MANSION

A wealthy merchant
entertains his guests.
They sit at a low
table.

Olives

Grapes were crushed
to make wine.

INSIDE THE KITCHEN

Pot of vegetable stew

Bread baked in a beehive-shaped oven

A calf roasting on a spit

Most households ground their own flour.

The servants are dressed alike and are ready to obey any orders.

Water collected daily

Bread

Fish caught from lakes and rivers

Households grew their own vegetables, including onions, leeks and beans.

The road to Jerusalem

Luke 19

It was getting close to Passover time. Jesus had set his
heart on being in Jerusalem for the festival. Even though
many of the religious leaders hated him, he was not
going to be put off from going.

At last he and his disciples reached the Mount of
Olives. The city was just across the valley.

Jesus announced that he wanted to ride the rest of the
way, and he sent two of his disciples to fetch a donkey.

Then, as the afternoon sun began to sink, Jesus climbed on the animal and began to lead the way down the hill.

The road to Jerusalem was busy with pilgrims. Someone noticed that the man on the donkey was Jesus. 'Look!' he whispered to his companion. 'It looks as if the preacher is going to declare he's really someone at last!'

'Let's give him a cheer,' said the other.

'God bless the king! God bless the king!' they shouted.

At once, others joined in. Excitement spread through the gathering crowd. In no time at all Jesus was being given a hero's welcome, with people cutting palm branches and waving them like victory flags.

Among the crowd were some Pharisees. They marched up to Jesus in a state of indignation.

'Teacher!' they said. 'Tell your followers to stop this nonsense at once.'

'I could tell them to keep quiet,' he said, 'but that wouldn't change the way things are.'

He rode closer to the city. 'Poor old Jerusalem,' he said to himself. 'You don't know what is needed for peace. You're going to miss your chance, and then all your fine buildings will be destroyed.' Suddenly, he felt overwhelmingly sad, and a tear ran down his cheek.

Then he went through the city gate and into the Temple courtyard. The noise was deafening: the place had been turned into a market.

'What do you think you're doing?' he accused a stallholder. 'The Temple is meant to be a house of prayer.'

'There's business to be done,' came the answer, 'for the Passover ceremonies. I can give you an excellent

exchange rate on the Temple coins. My cousin is
selling the pigeons you'll need as an offering, and if
you trade with me he'll give you his best rate as well.'

Jesus glared at him, then pushed his table over.
Moments later, he was marching round the courtyard
and driving everyone out.

In Jerusalem

The Temple that Jesus knew was built by King Herod. He governed the land on behalf of the Romans at the time Jesus was born.

The Mount of Olives

The olive grove called Gethsemane

Temple

Antonia Fortress

The route Jesus travelled from Bethany to Jerusalem on Palm Sunday.

The palace that King Herod had built. Later, the Roman governor Pontius Pilate used it as his official residence.

The hill of Golgotha, where Jesus was crucified.

A festival meal

Luke 22

The festival week slipped by. Jesus spent long hours preaching and teaching in the Temple.

Not far away, one of Jesus' disciples had business of his own. He knew only too well that the religious leaders were eager to arrest Jesus so they could silence him. He knew they were looking for a chance to do so quietly... and he, Judas, had decided to help them.

He saw a priest hurrying away from his turn of duty, and went to whisper to him. The man

nodded slowly, then ushered him through a doorway
and into a low-ceilinged room. A messenger was sent
to fetch others. Soon, the chief priests and officers of
the Temple guard filed their way in. They talked
tactics and timing. They talked money. A deal was
struck.

The rest of Jesus' disciples knew nothing. They
were looking forward to the Passover meal.

One of Jesus' supporters who
lived in Jerusalem had
agreed to lend them an
upstairs room. Peter
and John were given
the task of getting
everything
ready.

When the time came, Jesus took his place at the table with the disciples. 'I've been looking forward to this,' he announced. He explained that the great task he had begun was about to enter a new stage.

The disciples were used to Jesus saying puzzling things. By now they were eager to get on with the eating and drinking. They had grown up with the Passover traditions: the meal itself was celebrated with special foods and special prayers. The story of the first Passover had to be retold, and then everyone remembered the time of Moses and the great agreement their people had made with God: the great covenant that God was their God and they were God's people.

Then, quietly and purposefully, Jesus began to give new meaning to the old traditions. He took a piece of bread, gave thanks to God, shared the bread with his disciples and said, 'This is my body, which is given for you. Do this in memory of me.'

After supper he took the ceremonial cup of wine and shared it round.

'Listen,' he said. 'This cup is God's new covenant, sealed with my blood, which is poured out for you.'

It was a moment of great solemnity.

When the evening drew to a close, the men walked out into the darkness. They had already chosen the sheltered olive grove known as Gethsemane as the place where they could lie down and sleep.

Only Jesus stayed awake, praying to God for strength to deal with what lay ahead.

And then Judas arrived. 'Ah! I knew I'd find you all here,' he said, and he gave Jesus the kiss of greeting.

Jesus shook his head sadly. 'So that's the signal you chose to give to betray me,' he said. 'I can see your companions already.'

All around, armed men stepped out of the shadows. They closed in on Jesus, not bothered that the other disciples were running for their lives.

The soldiers arrested Jesus and marched him to the house of the high priest. There were hours to go before morning. The soldiers amused themselves by bullying their prisoner: they blindfolded him, beat him and insulted him.

Then, when it was day, they hustled Jesus into the room where the chief priests and the teachers of the Law had assembled.

'So,' said the priest in charge, and his tone was severe, 'are you the messiah, the Christ, God's chosen king?'

Jesus knew they had already decided what to do with him. There was nothing he could say to make them change their minds.

Three great festivals

The best place for the Jews to celebrate the ancient festival of Passover was in Jerusalem. There were special ceremonies at the Temple there.

A PASSOVER MEAL

This festival recalled the time when Moses led the people of Israel out of Egypt. On that night, the people of Israel prepared a special meal: a roast lamb and bread baked without yeast. By the time of Jesus, their meal had developed its own traditions, including special prayers.

The youngest child traditionally asks the oldest member of the family what they are celebrating.

Wine

A herb salad

Bread

PENTECOST

Pentecost came fifty days after Passover. It celebrated the grain harvest festival. After he received God's Holy Spirit, Peter preached about Jesus' resurrection to Pentecost pilgrims from all over the empire.

Gathering corn into sheaves.

ATONEMENT

The Day of Atonement was a time for the people to say sorry to God for their wrongdoing. Like all the major festivals, it was announced by priests sounding a blast on the ram's horn trumpet – the shofar.

Young and old take part in the festival.

The crucifixion

Luke 23; John 18–19

The Roman who had been appointed governor of Jerusalem was a man named Pontius Pilate. He did not have a great deal of interest in the religious traditions of the people he ruled.

He listened wearily as the chief priests told him about their prisoner.

'He's leading our people astray. He's telling people not to pay taxes. He's claiming to be the messiah – that's our word for king.'

Pilate questioned Jesus himself.

He's no threat to me or to Rome, he thought to himself. My choice would be to release him.

The priests were dismayed at his decision. They argued their case back and forth till Pilate knew he had to put an end to all their nonsense.

'All right,' he said. 'I'll have him whipped, and then let him go.'

He glanced outside. 'Look!' he added. 'The crowds are gathering. It's time for me to release a prisoner as a Passover privilege. I'm sure they'll want Jesus – he has been popular, hasn't he! I'll go and ask right now.'

But the crowd outside had other ideas. Their hero was a well-known rebel, and they chanted his name: 'Barabbas! Barabbas!'

Pilate looked down in astonishment, and lifted his hand for quiet. 'What shall I do with Jesus?' he asked.

'Crucify him! Crucify him!' they screamed.

The anger of the crowd made Pilate nervous. He was afraid they might riot if he didn't give them what they wanted.

'Well,' he announced, 'Barabbas goes free; Jesus gets the death sentence. I'll give my officers the order at once.'

Jesus was marched away. The soldiers loaded a great beam of wood onto his shoulders. 'You carry your own cross,' they laughed. 'And you've got company: there are two more who have to make that short but memorable walk to Calvary Hill.'

When they reached the rocky hill just outside the city walls, they nailed Jesus to the wood of his cross and hung him up to die. The two criminals were nailed to their crosses on either side.

Jesus looked down as the soldiers began to share out his possessions. He looked at the respectable people who had plotted to have him put to death. He said a prayer: 'Father, forgive them. They don't know what they are doing.'

For three hours Jesus hung on the cross. The noonday sun slid behind a shadow and the sky went dark. People came to stare at the executions. Some jeered. Others wept – among them the women who had followed Jesus and who still believed in him.

Then Jesus cried out: 'Father, in your hands I place my spirit.'

And then he died.

Not long after, a man named Joseph arrived with a little group of helpers.

He had been given permission to take Jesus' body. He and his companions were going to give Jesus a decent burial. Not far away, a rock-cut tomb was ready.

They loaded the body onto a funeral stretcher and carried it away. Some of the women who had followed Jesus from Galilee came too.

The mourners did not have much time. The sun was sinking low in the sky. Its setting would mark the beginning of the sabbath day of rest.

Hurriedly, Jesus' body was wrapped and placed in the tomb. The women watched to see what was done

before the stone door was rolled shut.

'We'll come back after the sabbath to wrap the body properly,' they agreed, 'and then we can use the traditional spices and perfumes as well.'

Then the sun touched the horizon line. The clouds went red for a few moments and then faded to grey.

Night-time was upon them all.

A *funeral*

Death is the natural ending of life, and the people of the Bible accepted it as such. However, the body needed to be dealt with respectfully and, in a hot climate, speedily. Those left behind were expected to grieve.

The body is carried on a stretcher to the place of burial.

There is wailing and mournful music.

The tomb is a cave in a rock. Its stone door can be rolled shut.

OSSUARY
Once the body had rotted, the bones were put in an ossuary – a bone box.

The body is washed and wrapped in strips of cloth.

Anointing oil

Ossuary

Mourners wear sackcloth and ashes.

The body was taken to a cave cut in rock. A tomb like this had space for several bodies and ossuaries.

Sunday morning

Luke 24

It was very early on Sunday morning. The sky was only just turning pale as the day dawned.

The women who had believed so much in Jesus were already on their way to his tomb. They wanted to complete the funeral traditions in the very best way they could. It would their way of saying a last goodbye.

'It's going to be quite hard for us to move the stone door, isn't it?' said one. 'There were more helpers when it was rolled shut. Do you think we'll manage?'

'It was a very large stone,' said another. 'It's bound to be really heavy.'

'Isn't it strange what you imagine in this half light,'

said a third, whose name was Mary Magdalene. 'It looks from here as if the stone door has been rolled away.'

As they came nearer they all slowed to a stop and gazed at one another in amazement.

'The stone really has been rolled away,' said Mary. 'Who can have done that?'

Their eyes were full of fear. Who had moved the stone? And if the tomb was wide open, what might have happened to Jesus' body?

Warily, they walked closer.

Clutching one another, they bent to look inside the tomb.

It was empty.

The women stepped back. Their thoughts were racing. Who had been at the tomb before them? Was that person still close by?

A slight noise made them whirl round. There were two men – no one they knew, or even like anyone they knew – standing quietly. Their tunics were shining white.

The women gasped in fear and bowed low.

'Why are you looking in a tomb for someone who is

alive?' said one of the men. 'He isn't here – God has
raised him to life.'

The women glanced at one another. Then they
simply turned and ran.

They ran all the way to where the disciples were
still in hiding – only eleven now that Judas had
disappeared.

The women had hardly got indoors before they
began to scream their news. 'Jesus! His body's gone!'
they cried. 'There were people at the tomb – angels
maybe – who said he was alive. You have to come
and see!'

The disciples simply stared at them.

'You're upset,' said one sullenly. 'But there's no
need to talk nonsense.'

Only Peter decided to go and see for himself. He
found the empty tomb and the grave clothes that had
been wrapped round Jesus. He didn't know what to
think.

The surprise guest

Luke 24

The news about Jesus' empty tomb was not
something that anyone dared to talk about openly;
even so, it spread like wildfire among the people who
believed in Jesus. It found its way into every
whispered conversation.

Two of them were still talking about the strange
news as they set off for home that evening. They lived
in Emmaus, just a few hours' walk from Jerusalem.

As they walked and talked, another person came along the same road. He was going the same way, and they began to make conversation.

'I notice you're looking rather unhappy,' said the stranger. 'What were you talking about that makes you feel that way?'

'Haven't you heard?' they replied. 'We were talking about Jesus of Nazareth. He was a preacher – a prophet even – and he had many followers, including us. But the religious leaders didn't like him and they had him crucified.

'His terrible, cruel death was bad enough. But now the news has taken a very strange twist. Some women

went to his tomb – and they found it was open and the body had gone. They talked some nonsense about angels saying that Jesus was alive, but that sort of thing doesn't happen. This is the real world, after all.'

The stranger thought a moment before speaking. 'It does make sense really,' he said. 'Our holy books talk about the messiah, after all, and they do say that he will have to suffer before his kingdom really comes into being.'

'Explain more!' the two insisted; and the stranger began to talk.

He went on talking all the way to Emmaus, and they were eager to go on listening.

'Come and stay with us,' they pleaded. 'It's getting dark. You'll need somewhere to stay the night.'

The man agreed. They all went into the house and prepared a simple meal.

When they all sat down to eat, the man took the bread in his hands to say the blessing prayer. Then he broke it into pieces for all of them to share.

As he did so, the two people recognized who it was. 'It's you! It's Jesus!' they exclaimed.

But all at once, he was gone.

The two didn't even stop to finish their meal. They got up and almost ran the miles back to Jerusalem.

They went straight to the place where the eleven disciples were staying.

To their astonishment, the group was in an exuberant mood. 'Jesus has risen from the dead!' the disciples told them. 'Simon has actually seen him!'

'Well, so have we!' they replied. And they told their story about the walk home and the moment when Jesus broke the bread.

While they were speaking, Jesus came and stood among them.

His appearance was such a surprise, they almost fainted.

'Why start doubting now!' laughed Jesus. 'I'm not a ghost. Look, my hands and feet show the marks of nails. Touch me – you'll find out I'm flesh and blood. And more than that, I'm ready for something to eat. What have you got? Fish? That will be nice.'

As he ate, he began to explain what was going on:

God's promises were coming true. The time had come to welcome everyone in the world to be part of God's kingdom and to live as one of God's people.

God's own Spirit

Luke 24; Acts 1–2

Jesus' followers had no doubts left: they truly believed he had risen from the dead.

However, his work on earth was done. It was time for him to return to heaven.

He led his followers to a village outside Jerusalem.

'The task I began is yours to continue,' he told them. 'Don't begin at once: you must wait until God fills you with the Holy Spirit. It will give you the strength and wisdom you need. Then you will spread the message that I taught you. You will take it to every corner of the world.'

Then he said a blessing prayer. As he did so, he was taken up into heaven. A cloud hid him from their sight.

They were still looking up when two men dressed in white came and stood next to them.

'Why are you looking up at the sky?' they asked.

'Jesus has gone to heaven. One day, he will return.'

Fifty days after Passover came a harvest festival
called Pentecost. Once again, Jerusalem was full of
pilgrims. The disciples had decided to stay indoors:
they were still wary of the religious leaders.

Suddenly they heard a noise. It was like a strong
wind blowing all through the house. Bright golden
flames began to swirl and dance above them and
touched each and every one.

They felt strangely different: confident and joyful.
They knew in their hearts that God had filled them
with the Holy Spirit.

Then the joy bubbled up within them as words
they simply had to say. They found they were

speaking different languages, and they laughed with amazement and delight before rushing out into the street to talk to anyone and everyone.

The pilgrims who had come to Jerusalem from faraway places were astonished. 'Listen to those people! They look as if they come from Galilee, but they're talking our language.

'And listen to the amazing things they're saying: that God has done great things. This is all rather odd.'

Not everyone was convinced. 'You're all drunk,' some shouted at the disciples. 'Stop making a nuisance of yourselves.'

Peter stood up and began to speak. His voice rang
out loud and clear. Everyone had to stop and listen.

'I ask you all to understand what's going on,' he
said. 'God's Holy Spirit has changed us. It's a sign

that all of God's promises are coming true.

'The most important thing to know is about Jesus. The leaders here in Jerusalem put him to death. God raised him to life. God has made him the greatest king there ever was and ever will be. He is the messiah, the Christ.'

The people in the crowd were astonished and rather worried. 'Is God really doing powerful things in the world?' they asked. 'If so, what should we do to be safe?'

Peter was ready with an answer. 'Turn away from wrongdoing. Be baptized in the name of Jesus Christ. God will forgive all that is past and fill you with the Holy Spirit. You will be a child of God.'

On that day, 3,000 more people became believers. They all supported one another as they learned to live as followers of Jesus.

From Jerusalem to all the world

Acts; 1 Corinthians

The religious leaders in Jerusalem were furious.

'The things that Jesus said and did were nothing but trouble!' they said. 'We've managed to get rid of him – and now his followers start causing even more mayhem.

'There is even talk that they are performing miracles of healing. Some lame beggar is leaping around saying that Peter made him well enough to walk again.

'And, of course, there are the thousands of people who are flocking to be part of their community. We must stamp on this new movement at once.'

So they began a campaign of seeking out the leaders and

putting them in jail. One young believer, Stephen, was cruelly put to death.

Leading the campaign against the followers of Jesus was a scholar named Saul. The believers learned to fear him because he was ruthless in tracking them down and putting them in jail.

When many of the believers fled Jerusalem, Saul set off to find them in other cities.

He was on his way to Damascus when something
astonishing happened. A light from the sky flashed
all around him.

As he fell to the ground he heard a voice: 'Saul!
Why are you treating me so cruelly?'

'Who are you?' shouted Saul.

'I am Jesus,' said the voice. 'Now, get up and go to
Damascus, and you will find out what to do next.'

When Saul opened his eyes, he found he could not see. His companions led him to the city and made sure he was safe.

Meanwhile in Damascus, a believer whose name was Ananias had a special dream. In the dream, God told him to go and find Saul and heal his blindness.

Ananias was very wary of Saul. He had heard tales of the cruel things he had done. However, he was not going to disobey God.

He went to Saul. 'It is really Jesus who sent me to you,' he said. 'The same Jesus who spoke to you on the road. Jesus wants me to heal your sight. Then God will fill you with the Holy Spirit.'

Everything happened as Ananias said. Saul had a complete change of heart. He was no longer an enemy of the believers. Instead, he was a believer himself.

With Saul on their side, life became a little easier for the believers. They preached the news about Jesus and the kingdom of God wherever they could.

One day, Peter had a special dream, and in his dream he understood that God was telling him something new. The message about Jesus wasn't just for his own people, the Jews. It was for everyone.

Peter himself began by preaching the news to a Roman centurion. He and his household all became believers.

Saul set off on a long journey across part of the Roman empire to spread the message.

He became better known by the Roman form of his name – Paul – and set up many new groups of believers.

Even though he did not stay very long in one place, he kept in touch by writing letters. What he wrote was full of wise teaching and encouragement.

'Three things are important to those of us who believe in Jesus,' he wrote. 'They are faith, hope and love. The greatest of these is love.'

The message about Jesus always spoke of love: about loving God and about loving one another.

Even so, Paul and the other disciples faced all kinds of dangers as they went about their work. Sometimes they were arrested and whipped. Sometimes they were thrown in jail. They knew that their enemies would be happy to see them executed.

But their faith in Jesus did not waver. God's Holy Spirit gave them all the hope and encouragement they needed.

When Paul made his last great journey, which was to the great city of Rome, he found that there were groups of believers already thriving.

The message that Jesus had first preached in Galilee had reached throughout the Roman empire and to its very centre.

There was no doubt it would spread everywhere.

Paul's travels

People could travel easily through the Roman empire. The Romans controlled the sea routes; the Roman roads were straight and well paved.

MAP OF PAUL'S JOURNEYS

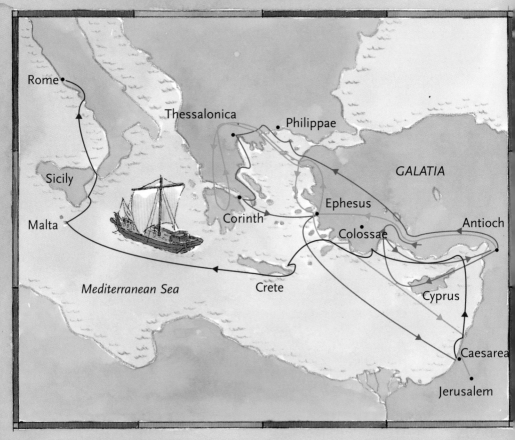

Rome

Thessalonica

Philippae

Sicily

GALATIA

Malta

Ephesus

Corinth

Colossae

Antioch

Mediterranean Sea

Crete

Cyprus

Caesarea

Jerusalem

— Paul's first journey   Paul's second journey   Paul's third journey

— Paul's journey to Rome

Paul climbs aboard a cargo ship to travel to different places in the Roman empire.

Heaven and earth

Revelation 21

John sighed. It was hard work in the prison camp. He had been arrested because he believed in Jesus. Now he spent his days quarrying stone.

When he wasn't working, God gave him dreams.

'One day,' he wrote, 'I saw a new heaven and a new earth. I saw a holy city – the new Jerusalem. It was built of gold and jewels, and was the loveliest place there could ever be.

'I heard a voice speaking. "God's home is now with human beings," it said. "God will truly be their God. They will truly be God's people. There will be no more death or crying or pain."

'And Jesus told me this: "Listen! I am coming soon. Does anyone long to be part of this new kingdom? Come, and drink from its fountain; drink the water of life."'